REBOOTING CLAUSEWITZ

CHRISTOPHER COKER

Rebooting Clausewitz

'On War' in the Twenty-First Century

HURST & COMPANY, LONDON

First published in the United Kingdom in 2017 by
C. Hurst & Co. (Publishers) Ltd.,
41 Great Russell Street, London, WC1B 3PL
© Christopher Coker, 2017
All rights reserved.
Printed in the United Kingdom

The right of Christopher Coker to be identified as the author
of this publication is asserted by him in accordance with the
Copyright, Designs and Patents Act, 1988.

A Cataloguing-in-Publication data record for this book
is available from the British Library.

ISBN: 9781849047142

This book is printed using paper from registered sustainable
and managed sources.

www.hurstpublishers.com

For My Students

CONTENTS

REASSURING COMMENTS ON CLAUSEWITZ FROM
THE DEPARTMENT OF DEFENSE TO THE HOUSE
APPROPRIATIONS COMMITTEE THURSDAY
13 MARCH 1997

SECURITY ASSISTANCE FOUND AT URL:
http://commdocs.house.gov/committees/approps/hapfop-par2.000/hapfoppar2_0.HTM

Mr Callahan: Thank you very much. What is it when you say, 'to paraphrase Clausewitz'? What is that? What is Clausewitz?

Mr Slocombe (Under Secretary of Defense for Policy): Clausewitz said that war is the continuation of policy by other means. I believe for the kind of programs which support our interests by non-military methods that are involved in this bill are the expression of national strategy by other means. These are not hand-outs to foreign countries as an act of charity.

Mr Callahan: Well, you'll have to forgive me.

Mr Slocombe: I apologise for the analogy, which is obscure.

Mr Callahan: Well, I mean, I never heard of Clausewitz. Maybe I haven't studied my history sufficiently.

Mr Slocombe: Clausewitz was a German general who...

Mr Callahan: I figured that.

Mr Slocombe: The book, I have to say, is impenetrable, but I think the only part of it which anybody has read is the one line that, 'war is the continuation of policy by other means.'

LIFE STORY

CARL PHILIPP GOTTLIEB VON CLAUSEWITZ

Born: 1 July 1780. **Died:** Aged 51 on 16 November 1831.

Educated: 1792—Prussian Army. Saw combat at the age of 13.

Marital Status: Married 1810 to Countess Marie von Brühl.

Works: *On War;* various essays.

Influences: Kant, Hegel? Scharnhorst.

Claims of Plagiarism: From Otto August Rühle von Lilienstern.

Movie appearances: *The Jaywalkers* (1959), *Cross of Iron* (1977), *Crimson Tide* (1995), *Monty Python and the Holy Grail* (1975), *Lions for Lambs* (2007).

His Admirers Say:

'Remembering Clausewitz makes you take your own thoughts a little less seriously.' (Bob Dylan, 2004)

His Critics Say:

'Enough! It is time to hold a wake so that strategists can pay their respects to Clausewitz and move on leaving him to rest among the historians.' (Steven Metz, 1994)

He Says:

'Half against my will I have become a Professor.' (Paret 2015, p. 100)

The Best Thing Said About Him:

'Clausewitz is not holy writ, only canon law.' (Colin Gray)

PROLOGUE—WHY THIS BOOK?

Clausewitz to go

A group of students discussing Clausewitz around a seminar table:

> Student A: *Oh, for Christ's sake, not Clausewitz again? He is a historical fossil—it's all Napoleon worship and decisive battles and Great Power wars. It is all so retro.*
>
> Student B: *But who else is there?*
>
> Student A: *Well there is Sun Tzu. And the future belongs to the Chinese doesn't it? Who wants to read what a nineteenth century German has to write about war.*
>
> Student C: *And try reading his book. It's so long.*
>
> Student B: *Yeah, and what's with all the fuss the professors make about his theory? It is not as though it is focussed. .... like, it's all over the place.*
>
> Student C: *Anyway, if he is so fucking smart why is he so fucking dead?*

OK, I have made this dialogue up; I didn't overhear it, but I might have done. I have heard all of these objections in the space of thirty-five years of teaching (though they tend to be voiced more often these days). And perhaps the conversation is more than a little contrived. Intellectually, these imagined students are clearly not the sharpest tools in the box but they are not entirely unrepresentative of student opinion either. TL, DR: 'Too Long, Didn't Read' is the *cri de coeur* of student life as professors know from many other disciplines. And *On War* is a very long book. Clausewitz's stodgy sentences don't always translate themselves from the nineteenth century page to the twenty-first century mind with ease. Besides which, if a reader and author have to coexist, we are cut off from one another by differing and often mutually exclusive perceptions of the world—overcome only, if at all, through enormous imaginative effort.

And what of the last line of my imagined dialogue (the killer argument for our sceptical young student)? Some readers will recall that it appears in John Huston's 1985 film *Prizzi's Honor*. The remark is made about a dead hit-man; what has it got to do with a writer who has been dead for nearly two centuries? Don't dead authors appear on university syllabuses all the time even when there are moves, as there are at my own, to update the courses? For many students who find the 'canon' too dated or boring, a writer's personal check-out date is almost equivalent to the sell-by date of his greatest work. The question the student should have asked is this: if a writer is long since dead, how smart is it of us to continue reading him? Although such thinking might be considered intensely shallow if we are discussing the great works of fiction, when it comes to non-fiction even the great books tend to have a much more limited shelf-life. Moreover in the case of war in which people really do end up dead then the question is not quite as outlandish as it may seem. What does a superannuated nineteenth century Prussian general still have to tell us about the wars we fight today?

It is also a mark of the times to build people up and then tear them down. Reputations come and go; celebrities quickly fall out of fashion. It is the norm to treat even our most revered contemporary writers as celebrities who one day will eventually fall out of fashion, and to dismiss works of the past as 'classics' in need of revision. 'Roll over Clausewitz,' wrote one so-called expert in an endorsement of a book by Martin Shaw, *The New Western Way of Warfare* (2005). A rather surprising endorsement, to be sure, since the actual author of the book went to great lengths to show how Clausewitz was still a central figure for any serious student of war. And there is a reason why this is the case. Nobody does science by reading Newton (though in Clausewitz's day they did). But we still assign *On War* at military academies, and university courses like my own because we still set out to identify the enemy's 'centre of gravity', and still talk of 'the grammar of war', and the challenge of 'friction'. All these are terms that Clausewitz introduced into the academic language of war; they are part of our common inheritance.

And he has been read by our enemies too, though we might ask how much they really understand him. A copy of *On War* was found in the

Tora Bora cave complex which once housed Osama Bin Laden, though his reading also included *The Grappler's Guide to Sports Nutrition* and his video library (much more usefully, as it turned out) included a guide to the American Special Forces video game, *Delta Force: Xtreme 2*. Bin Laden apparently spent his last years mostly watching porn sites. Hitler's library did include Clausewitz, right enough, but it also included a complete set of the novels of Karl May, a popular writer of American style cowboy and Indian stories at the turn of the twentieth century. Hitler chose to despatch these third-rate Westerns (not *On War*) to his generals on the Eastern Front in the hope of inspiring them to continue the fight—for which, of course, we must be eternally grateful (Macintyre, 2015).

There is a more interesting point at issue. Hitler once claimed that everything he had learned about politics he had learned from reading *On War* (not quite the ringing endorsement any self-respecting author would want). Whether Hitler even read him is still debated—he was given a copy of the book when he was in the Landsberg prison in the early 1920s. But his reference to Clausewitz in *Mein Kampf* is to the *Denkschriften* of 1912. Just because someone says that they have read an author of course, doesn't mean that they have read him as he would wish to be read—all language is corruptible for that reason. As the playwright Denis Potter once complained: 'the trouble with words is that you don't know whose mouth they have been in.' If Hitler did read *On War* he clearly did not read it closely enough; he read into it what he wanted. His career may afford a vivid example of how the misreading of a text can feed back into history and help shape its course.

So, you can see why I am not entirely unsympathetic to students who question the continuing 'relevance' of a great work, even if they are not especially well-informed. And at military colleges across the United States, there must be cadets who wonder whether being on familiar terms with a Prussian General who lived 180 years ago is really going to be much help in their careers; some may even question whether war lends itself to theorising. But then it really does. Take the story of one young cadet at the US Navy War College who asked the then Chairman of the Joint Chiefs of Staff after a lecture he delivered in 2002 what was the nature of the war they were still fighting in Afghanistan. The young man had read that Clausewitz tells us never to engage in a war unless you understand its true nature. The response of General Franks was revealing: 'It's a good question, son, but don't ask me, ask the historians' (Ricks, 2012, 400). There was a general who never read Clausewitz, or perhaps more to the point, never understood him. The unspoken implication of the general's response is that theories are for fools. And there is certainly no point theorising for its own sake. Abstract thinking does not always help you achieve your objectives. But at its best it offers the chance of turning a tactical success into a conclusive strategic outcome (something that Franks failed to do, not only in Afghanistan but also in Iraq one year later).

So let me cut to the chase. I set out to write this book because of the question asked by my real as opposed to fictional students—why does Clausewitz still matter? And if he really is as 'relevant' as ever, how is this possible? How can a book written almost 200 years ago still be useful? Perhaps, it is a mistake to volunteer an answer before I have had time to develop my main arguments. But students are impatient with their professors these days; they like to know where they are heading the better to grasp where they are coming from. So if you ask why we are still reading the work of a nineteeth century Prussian general, the answer is that he knew more about war than anyone else, and he also knew more than he realised, as I hope to show in this book.

The book's title—*Rebooting Clausewitz*—does not mean, as many may think it does, 'revamping', 'rebranding', or 'recycling'. It means quite the opposite. It means showing how he got there first; how recent understandings have tended to bear him out. We owe that to Clausewitz's own open-mindedness. He was constantly reframing questions, revising his text, changing his mind, even accepting that he was sometimes at a loss to explain certain realities. What I would claim is that his influence has eclipsed his originality—*On War* is full of intuitive insights that neither his contemporaries nor subsequent generations could appreciate for what they were; now, we can.

So what's the problem?

There is a problem that we need to confront head-on. At a conference in Stockholm a few years ago Martin van Creveld gave a paper on 'The Crisis of Military theory.' He began by reminding his audience that there has been no shortage of writing on war, and some of the writers have been inspired. One who is often forgotten is Vegetius (a late Roman writer who was the main influence in medieval Europe—recently rediscovered by historians [Morillo]); another was Machiavelli whose *Art of War* was once a staple of military institutes (thanks to the popularity of *The Prince* he is now, like Clausewitz, largely a one-book author). And then there is a range of twentieth century authors also largely known only to specialists, such as the French writer, André Beaufre. Ultimately, they have all failed to make the cut because they focussed too much on their own times. Clausewitz survives, not because his work is timeless but because it is not entirely rooted in his own time.

Even then, van Creveld argued, there are large gaps—he expresses no interest in why wars are fought (one of the main topics of Thucydides' *History*). And you won't find any discussion of cyber warfare, war in Low Earth Orbit, nuclear weapons, or even economics, or for that matter technology which now largely determines how we fight. I shall argue that the last criticism isn't necessarily true but one can hardly dispute the other elements of the case for the prosecution. Clausewitz, he insists, can no longer be of much value to today's students. *On War* can no longer do for students what a theory should—save them the need to think out everything from the beginning (van Creveld, 2015, 71).

Van Creveld happens be one of the few major theorists of war in the world today—the list is not a long one—so what he says must be taken seriously. Another major writer, the military historian John Keegan, also spent much of his life condemning what he liked to label the 'military Leninists'—the top Clausewitzian scholars—for telling their students that Clausewitz had said all there was to say on the subject of war, a claim by the way that the general never made himself (Keegan, 1997, 5). Keegan was unfair; van Creveld, I think, is far too despairing, but does he have a point? Another writer who also takes Clausewitz to task for his theoretical 'incoherence' attributes it to his method—his distinction (probably derived from Kant) between the ideal (noumenal) and the real (phenomenal) worlds which encouraged him to make statements about the first which he knew reality could not back up (Fleming 2004).

In rebuttal I would ask: why should a student fully expect to understand any theoretical work on first reading? A first year physics student is not expected to be entirely at home with quantum mechanics. Modern theoretical models in physics may have become more complex but that doesn't discourage teachers from insisting that their students try to understand first principles. War may be less complex than the idea of string theory but it is complex enough—it would be surprising if writing about it were any more instantly comprehensible. Yet that is not the real problem, of course. One of the challenges I find in persuading students that Clausewitz's work is still important is that these days they don't indeed want to know how to think, but what to think about everything including war. *The Art of War* is to be found in the business sections of many airport bookshops, *On War* isn't. Businessmen too are in a hurry; they read abstracts of papers rather than the papers in full and of course they make money by telling their clients what to think, not how to think. Wisdom is not about knowledge but method. Keep in mind a bit of gnomic wisdom from the linguist Ann Farmer: 'It isn't about being right. It is about getting it right.' (Pinker, 2012, 303). I like to tell my own students that Clausewitz is worth reading precisely because he is so difficult, even if there probably is a market for a book called *Clausewitz for Dummies*.

The Book

As the title of *On War* suggests, it is a book addressing itself to a big theme; its ambition is unmistakeable. Clausewitz tried to capture what he called the 'mystery of war' and he succeeded, but only up to a point. There are longueurs to be sure but there is rarely a moment when you don't feel that a sophisticated intelligence is at work. In the end it is less the subject itself that compels admiration than the author's willingness to tackle one of the biggest themes of all from practically every angle. You have to admire the courage of a man who, in extending himself, was pushing against the limits of his own imagination and largely coming through.

We are lucky to have the work at all, however. Clausewitz died with it still unfinished. What if his widow hadn't persisted in getting it published? He is also reputed to have wanted to write a sequel—a companion volume on small wars. If this was the case (and the smart money is against it) it would be one of those sequels that never make it into print—like the planned *Encyclopaedia* of his once much more famous contemporary, the poet Novalis, which never saw the light of day thanks to his anxieties about whether the contents list would also serve as an index (Stuart, 2005, xix).

The regard in which its author has been held, however, is more recent in some countries than others. He was an established figure in the German staff college by 1880 thanks largely to the support of its most famous nineteenth-century Field Marshall, Helmut von Moltke. *On War* was already widely read in French translation before the First World War. But it did not become widely known in the United States until after the Second World War. So, if you care to think of *On War* as an entry for an American literary competition—say the Pulitzer Prize—then you could say that it would have been long-listed if it had been submitted in 1943; shortlisted by the 1960s and that its author would have carried off the prize in 1983—at which point they might have stopped awarding it, on the understanding that its author had set a standard that could never be matched.

So, what was Clausewitz up to; why did his book make waves? Here is one explanation. In 1949 the philosopher Gilbert Ryle proposed two knowledge categories: 'knowing what' and 'knowing why' (Ryle, 1949, 28). 'Knowing what' is the raw information, the data-sets, the information that we all need to navigate our way through the world. Every commander needs to know the geographical lie of the land; the resources of the enemy, as well as his own; the belief systems of those he is fighting (will they fight to the end, or can they be brought quickly to the negotiating table). 'Knowing why' is different; it is about turning 'tacit knowledge' (what we know over time from observation) into 'explicit knowledge' (what we know from science to be true). And that truth can be communicated across generations by translating it into laws, codes, or mathematical equations. Explicit knowledge is vital in war; it allows for an improvement in performance, which is why Clausewitz wrote his book. Access to knowledge, including intellectual capital, makes for better judgement and decision making. Thucydides was once credited with writing that a country that does not have thinking warriors will have its thinking done by fools and fighting by idiots.

If he didn't actually say it; he might well have. It is a sentiment that he certainly would have shared.

Perhaps, the best way to bring this home is to remind ourselves that Clausewitz's contemporaries did not always know the 'why' of things we take for granted. Think of Nelson standing on the deck of the *Victory* at the Battle of Trafalgar, tacking into the winds, but having no scientific understanding of how to measure them. Think of the young Turner who had no vocabulary to describe the clouds he painted, and no way of explaining how they stayed suspended in the air. Think of Mary Shelley who could write so vividly of a storm on the night of Victor Frankenstein's wedding, but had no scientific understanding of what a storm actually is. All three understood how, but not why. Nelson knew how sea battles could turn on winds. Turner knew his clouds, Constable even more so (he turned out hundreds of sketches in an attempt to understand them, and the infinite gradations of light that they produced). Shelley knew the importance of storms in the emotional build up in literature, but the 'how' continued to elude her, as it did all the others. But the 'how' was about to be discovered, beginning in 1802 when an Englishman devised the cloud classification that we know today (cirrus/cumulus). Goethe congratulated him for imposing 'order on chaotic nature' (Moore, 2015). And in a sense this is what Clausewitz set out to do with respect to our understanding of war.

It appears to be a deep human impulse. There is an orderly impulse in all of us; our structural quests for order can be grouped under the collective term 'structural intuitions'. 'The historical progression is from static patterns to orders that involve dynamism, process, fields of energy and the duality of waves and particles, moving decisively beyond the narrow observational span of the frequencies of light that we actually observe.' (Kemp, 2015). Clausewitz spent a lifetime asking the 'why' question—analysing war from all different angles, investigating the chaos. Thanks to a scientific method that stopped well short of claiming war could ever become a science, he moved us towards a more instrumental idea of conflict. He did not just record this transformation; to an extent he was instrumental in bringing it about.

So, the reader will find in the book everything—or almost everything—he wanted to know about war but was afraid to ask. The book's great value is that it offers us a clearing in a dense philosophical forest that few of us would have the ability or inclination to navigate alone. But it is not a breeze. It is certainly not a joy to read. In the long run, wrote Raymond Chandler, 'however little you talk or even think about it, the most durable thing in writing is style, and style is the most valuable investment a writer can make with his time' (James, 2013, 201). Agreed, Chandler was writing about fiction (think of all those Philip Marlowe one-liners), but the same applies to non-fiction as well, and no-one, not even his admirers, can claim that Clausewitz was one of the great stylists. He has his moments, there are a few poetic flashes, but touches of humour are notable by their complete absence and he rarely conveys the immediacy of human experience except in moments of autobiographical truth. One notable Clausewitz scholar, Hew Strachan, insists that *On War* does have its pithy phrases and memorable sayings which gain in strength precisely because they state the obvious (Strachan and Herberg-Rothe, 2007, 17). It is quite an arresting thought and it is one that I would ask you to keep in mind. *On War* is no better written, in fact, than it needed to be, but his main hold on us is definitely not through language.

And it is a long work—very long. This is not a challenge, of course, when it comes to Sun Tzu's *Art of War*. One of my former students, Thomas Rid, complains that Sun Tzu is all very well, but the *Art of War* reads at times like a choppy Twitter feed from 500 BC. Clausewitz offers a far more coherent 'tool set' for rigorous analysis (Rid, 2011, 1). But then what is a book but thousands of tweets printed out and stapled together between pieces of cardboard. The point is that Clausewitz's book is big by any standards. And more of a challenge now than ever before, in the age of the smart phone and limited attention spans.

But hold that thought for a moment. What do we mean by attention span? It is not what we often think—that multi-tasking, skimming and surfing the net reduces even the best student's capacity for concentration. The ability to keep something in the mind and to focus is no worse (or for that matter much better) than it probably was for the student body fifty years ago. Attention is so central to our ability to think, writes Daniel T. Willingham, that to suffer a significant loss would require the retro-fitting of other cognitive functions, and that will not happen (if it happens at all) for some time yet. It would actually constitute a marked evolutionary change. But it is possible that in the last twenty years our digital devices have made it less rewarding to concentrate for a long period of time, or to tackle a 500 page text. When reading something on the internet we are always asking ourselves whether something else might not be more interesting or entertaining. Willingham suggests that what is really happening is that we are more immersed in 'outward-directed' thought, a neuro-scientific term for what happens when we scroll down emails at the start of the morning, or when we play intensive video games at night. What tends to suffer, as a result, is 'inward-directed' thought, which includes reflection—a situation which he thinks is probably historically unprecedented (Willingham, 2015).

And that is a problem because we reflect for a purpose. It makes us more innovative, inventive and creative, all the qualities that the military seeks to draw out in its recruits. It is difficult to instil them, but it is possible to nurture them, and when you are about to go into battle it helps to have a theory of war, whether you wish to call it that or not.

Clausewitz: celebrity?

Were Clausewitz alive today he might also have completed his book. He left it incomplete at the time of his death from cholera at the age of 51—early by today's standards. Had he lived in the twenty-first century he could have expected to live a normal life span and have seen his book go into several editions. Perhaps his work would be raided by editors in search of an endless series of quotes. Perhaps while browsing airport bookshops we would find books with such titles as *Clausewitz's Six Leadership Lessons* or *Eight Lessons You Can Learn from Watching Clausewitz Teach a Class*. Perhaps, we would be able to follow his lectures on YouTube, or even read Tweets made up of strategic commentaries on today's events in the Greater Middle East.

When Walter Isaacson wrote the authorised 2011 life of Steve Jobs, there followed, among other works, *Ten Leadership Tips From Steve Jobs* (Forbes); *Six Management Lessons* (Globe & Mail); and *Fourteen Real Leadership Lessons*, drawn up by Isaacson himself for the *Harvard Business Review*. The Apple founder's death brought a remarkable life to a premature end, and the same could be said of Clausewitz, of course. As Jim Collins, the management writer told the authors of *Becoming Steve*

Jobs, had he lived beyond 55 the third phase of his life 'would have been fascinating; but we don't get to see that' (Hill, 2015), And we didn't get to see the third phase of Clausewitz's life either.

This is only one of several parallels between the two men's lives. The biography *Becoming Steve Jobs* narrates the evolution of its hero from the young Jobs 1.0, who lacked management skills, to Jobs 2.0, who managed to crack it on his return to Apple. One of the most obvious differences between Clausewitz 1.0, the soldier who found himself under fire at least thirty-three different times and Clausewitz 2.0, the author of *On War*, is that his time at the Academy made him a compelling theorist of war. The authors of the second Jobs biography argue that he was by the end of his life 'a business genius.' Similarly, Clausewitz ended his life a theoretical genius, whether he would have acknowledged the fact or not. While granting Jobs the same status as Edison and Henry Ford, Isaacson found that many people who worked with him also found him 'an asshole'. Well, not everyone found Clausewitz especially affable either, and not all his students found him an inspiring teacher; some of his contemporaries found him at bottom guarded, even unknowable.

Is all this impossibly whimsical? Possibly, but I don't think so. Clausewitz has constantly been imagined and re-imagined. He is not tied to his times, even if he reflects them. There are in fact several different versions of the man. There is the Clausewitz who Hitler says taught him all he knew. There is the Clausewitz who appealed to Engels (and was embraced by the Soviets). There is the 'Mahdi of Mass' who was excoriated by the English strategist Basil Liddell Hart. There is the sanitised, democratic Clausewitz which the US Army embraces on a highly selective reading of the text. There is Clausewitz the unimaginative Prussian officer and Clausewitz the romantic hero who broke out of the straitjacket of Prussian thinking, and to use today's term (which he probably would have abhorred) 'thought outside the box'.

He has gone through so many intellectual face-lifts that it is quite natural I think to project him into our own day and beyond. Were Clausewitz alive today, would he have become a strategy consultant to a government, or an employee of a think-tank like the RAND Corporation? Would he have yielded to his military side, his wish to 'do' rather than 'teach'? Here is another question: would he have moved to America and sought a teaching post at the National Defence

University (NDU) in Washington or the US Army War College? Would *On War* have been part of the 'publish or perish' culture, or his ticket to stardom and TV appearances?

The point of course was that in his age there were no celebrities or public intellectuals. Writers did not write to score points for their own pet concerns or beliefs. The fact is that no-one cared about his opinions at the time, which is why he was under no pressure to become opinionated. I suspect that were he alive today we would not find him satisfying the metrics of page-view 'clicks' and Facebook 'likes,' or attaining the maximum exposure of tweets and retweets in the hope that his message would eventually go viral. Yet he would still have much of value to tell us.

I was inspired to put pen to paper on this book after reading Rebecca Newberger Goldstein's book *Plato at the Googleplex* (2014) in which she set out to showcase the continuing relevance of the western world's foremost philosopher by bringing him back to life in the twenty-first century—mediating a debate between a psychoanalyst and a 'tiger mom' on how to raise the perfect child; visiting the Googleplex and coming to grips with the idea that knowledge can now be crowd-sourced rather than reasoned out by experts; and locking horns with a popular writer on a right-wing news show who denies that there can be morality without religion. I have tried to do the same with Clausewitz, a much less profound thinker, to be sure, but a man who still happens to be the best theorist in his own field of study. In addition to three essays situating Clausewitz in his time and ours, I have written three fictional encounters from a seminar at West Point and an evening debate on the War on Terror at a Washington think-tank, to an after-dinner talk at a rather stuffy Military History Circle in London.

Such endeavours inevitably run the risk of having one's seriousness of purpose cast into question. 'There is a fine line', wrote the Texas country and western singer Kinky Friedman, 'between fiction and non-fiction and I think I snorted it somewhere in 1979.' Whenever you are engaged in any thought-experiment you need to ensure that you remain within hailing distance of reality. But this is not the first exercise of its kind. The very first attempt at fictionalisation was spoof letters from Clausewitz on Mount Olympus written in the 1840s by one of his early admirers, Capt. von Pönitz, an officer in the army of Saxony. A further fictional interview with the general appeared in the late 1970s in the US Army's *Military Review* (Freudenberg, 1977). Another 'brief encounter' between Clausewitz and Jan Willem Honig, one of today's principal Clausewitzian scholars, appears in a book of 'interviews' with forty-one famous dead philosophers, including some who were deeply interested in war such as Plato, Aristotle and Machiavelli. In this version he appears as a crotchety old man (Honig, 2016, 126–133). We all have our own ideas of the man we would like to bring back to life. I prefer to imagine that he could walk into a seminar in West Point today and take part in a discussion with the cadets almost immediately. Doubtless, he would be surprised at how wired-in they are: checking their smartphones for emails, and Facebook pages to see that they do not miss out on any news, all the time being alert for the text messages that is their inheritance—their screen-based lifestyle. But what he would find familiar are the terms the students would use—such as 'centre of gravity', or their discussions on whether the nature of war is likely to change in future. He would also find familiar much of the setting of the Academy. The uniforms would not have changed that much, or the structure of military life.

But he would almost certainly be surprised to see women in uniform; and he would probably be horrified by the acronyms we now use. 'Great is the evil in the pompous retinue of technical terms', he wrote, and I have no doubt that he would almost certainly have hated our Power Point-driven unreality and the depressing *argot* of military life with its references to 'battle spaces', 'collateral damage', 'decapitation', 'payloads', 'non-lethal transfers', 'injections of risk', 'light footprints' and 'kinetic situations.' Even if he would understand the meaning, he would still hate the noise.

And how do we imagine Clausewitz himself would act in the presence of the young? I suspect he would have engaged with today's students, even if the relationship would have been much less formal, and in the words of his own generation, less 'correct'. I prefer to imagine that he would have liked to have been re-imagined not as a querulous old man, already at fifty ageing rapidly, impatient of the manners and mores of an era which sets such a premium on youth. I have chosen to re-imagine him as some of his friends preferred to remember him after his death—warm, if reticent, and not the unsmiling Prussian Staff

Officer who would later become a caricature towards the end of the nineteenth century.

I have chosen in the fictional interludes to this book to represent Clausewitz as he was known to his circle of friends. I like to think that he would have been proud to know how much of what he intuited has been borne out by recent research; he would have been proud to discover how the brand is still going strong. For our part we should stand amazed by what he was able to recognise through observation. What he frequently claimed to be true is now thanks to science a truth that is more in our possession than his. Unfortunately, we keep forgetting what he tried to tell us and are always having to re-learn the lessons when it is often too late.

1

CLAUSEWITZ AND HIS AGE

Should we be interested in a writer's life or just his life's work? Translating a writer's work into his life can be as perilous as translating his work into his life. The cardinal rule is surely this: the work and how it came into being is what it is worth writing about. The life should be invoked only to illuminate the work. Biography is the most popular form of history writing for the reason that we have a prurient interest in the murkier aspects of famous lives. But biographies are popular for another reason too: when we read a work of fiction or non-fiction we are interested—as Clausewitz's age was not—in the hidden authorial voice, and in what an author chooses to leave out. Especially those aspects of his personal experience that were supressed in his work, whether consciously or not. Every work is necessarily biographical. We now acknowledge that the world just doesn't reveal itself—we understand the world through our theories and social constructs in which deeply embedded are our unquestioned assumptions. We have to be on the look-out for an author's hidden biases, too, which are shaped by education, religion and values inculcated when young—many of which go unrecognised in the course of a life. So, although it is an oft-stated belief in some quarters that knowledge of a writer's personal life is of small relevance in helping us to understand his work, I think it is central to understanding Clausewitz's.

Clausewitz—The Biopic

On the cover of nearly every book on Clausewitz there is a famous portrait. We see a man of medium height and slight build, and rather aesthetic features, more a philosopher than a general. The mouth is not sensuous, but thin, and the chin clean-shaven for maximum exposure. The stare is rather inscrutable, offering no strong hint as to the emotional and psychological state of health of its subject. The portrait shows a serene man, not the Clausewitz some of his contemporaries knew—chippy, socially awkward at times, a troubled man who was perhaps too much the author of his own misfortunes? He was shy, reticent, and modest—a man who knew his own worth even though he also knew that he was under-valued.

George Orwell once claimed that by a certain age everyone gets the face they deserve. Martin Amis has updated this: these days some people get the face they can afford (Dyer, 2011, 19). What one can't escape is one's ethnic origins, and the one thing that may strike the viewer about the portrait is the fact that Clausewitz is what used to be called a Dead White European Male (DWEM). Being assigned to the category of course was not a sign of praise; it was invented as a declaration of irrelevance. But a new term has entered the lists: WEIRD—Western, Educated, Industrialised, Rich and Democratic. It has been persuasively argued that WEIRD people are the weirdest in the world—overwhelmingly male, white and educated into comparatively late age. Clausewitz only fits the bill when we invoke the first: he left school at 12 to join the army; Prussia was not yet industrialised and wouldn't be for some time; his family was not rich and, here's the real problem for some students, whatever his politics Clausewitz was not a democrat. There is no reason in fact to conclude that he would not have been in accord with the direction of German politics as the nineteenth century progressed.

If we cut down the bio to the basics here is what most scholars will tell you. He was the son of a retired army officer who had had an undistinguished role in the Seven Years' War. He came from a family that had fallen on hard and then harder times. Enlisting in the army at 12, he was promoted to Lance Corporal at 13, commissioned as an officer and promoted to the rank of Lieutenant two years later. He enrolled in the Berlin War Academy in 1801 where he first learned war from books and lectures. He was wounded in the 1806 war and spent some time as a Prisoner of War (POW) before becoming a professor at the War Academy. When Prussia was asked to join Napoleon's invasion of Russia he resigned his commission and joined the Russians. He was back in Prussian uniform by 1815 when the war resumed and was present at Waterloo. He spent his last years as Director of the War Academy where he worked on the book that made his name.

In other words, Clausewitz had a very varied experience of war, both as a Staff Officer and a soldier who was involved in a number of rear-guard actions and skirmishes in the Russian Campaign. He also helped organise popular resistance to the French in Prussia's Baltic provinces. His breadth of military experience was pretty unusual: it gave him the intellectual depth to see war from more than one vantage point.

Clausewitz in other words contained within himself many of the contradictions and battling impulses of his age. His innate conservatism was combined with barely concealed enthusiasm for the revolutionary fervour that carried French arms into battle. And since he was frequently critical of the German lack of spirit compared with the vigour of Revolutionary France, he would probably have been swept along by German nationalism. Like Hegel, he became increasingly conservative with age, and one writer suggests that in 1848 he might even have been found supporting the forces of reaction (Behrens, 1976). His early death is an open invitation to speculate about what he might have turned into but we certainly don't have to fashion a writer who would find himself at home at a Manhattan dinner party.

OK, let's try again. *Qui alios seipsum docet*—'He who teaches others, teaches himself'. In this case the Latin tag is not just a professorial indulgence. It captures what makes Clausewitz so unusual. He may well have learned something from exchanging views with his students, although there is little evidence for this and his teaching career ended early. At the War College to which he was appointed as Director in 1818 he wasn't allowed to put forward his theories or even to influence the training of the new officer corps. He seems to have withdrawn into himself shortly after his appointment. Such feelings of embattlement are the very qualities that he needed, perhaps, to fight against the orthodoxies of his day. He was a man struggling with a rather banal political and military culture without ever quite giving up on his own sense of self. In other words, he was the quintessential Romantic hero.

He spent much of his life trying to transcend his origins without disowning them. He complained that his father, and army friends among whom he had been brought up, had fallen in with the worst prejudices of their profession (Heuser, 1997, 1). He remained all his life at odds with the anti-intellectualism of the Prussian army. In the chapter on genius in Book I of *On War* he was particularly scornful of the resolute officer of the Hussars who is no deep thinker and is not given to self-questioning (you will find the type in the person of Colonel Feraud, the anti-hero of Joseph Conrad's novella *The Duellists*, and in a much more likeable form in Conan-Doyle's Brigadier Gerard (Coker, 2014). His conservatism became an essential plank in his later drive for radical reform. He wanted to bring war back to its 'true nature'; to reconnect the Prussian way of war with the core preoccupations that had been abandoned, or which he thought had been abandoned by the late eighteenth century. The Prussian is an indelible mark of Clausewitz's character. The term 'Prussian' here stands for the social and political world into which he was born, and its predominant achievement in its own social imagination, the art of war. He was to devote a lifetime trying to understand the forces shaping it, and through the pen, he was able to influence its future development.

It is really very difficult—as you can see—to sum up such a life. 'The intellect of man is forced to choose/Perfection of the life, or the work', W. B. Yeats wrote. In reality it is not that easy to disentangle the two. Clausewitz touched the two extremes of what life has to offer: the life of action and the life of contemplation. And for him there was no contradiction between the two, which is not true in the minds of most military men, both of his day and of our own. He believed that war had become the dominant theme of the age and that it behoved philosophy to study it. In a short note entitled 'On German philosophers with good intentions', he insisted that they should address the dominant realities of the day, that philosophy itself was an act of engagement, not an abstract indulgence (Engberg-Pedersen, 2015, 49). He came from a generation that was the very first to identify war as a problem of *knowledge* (Engberg-Pedersen, 2015, 3).

In short, he built three careers in one heroically productive life. First, from his early days in the Army he was an enterprising young officer who was deeply patriotic. After 1806 he turned that mission into reformist zeal to save the Prussian Army; he embarked on a mission to save his country from extinction. After 1815 he worked on the greatest book on war ever written. All his life he struggled against obstacles and *On War* must be seen in the context of that struggle. The book was really a life sentence. As Walter Benjamin once suggested, 'finished works are lighter than those fragments on which [authors] work throughout their lives.' (Coetzee, 2007, 40).

I call his life heroic because he persevered in the face of what some consider to have been failure in all three endeavours. Clausewitz saw very few set-piece battles. Apart from Borodino (1812) (he has a cameo part in Tolstoy's famous description of the battle) he was present at the Battle of Bautzen (1813) but not at the decisive battle—Leipzig (1813). During the Waterloo campaign he was at Wavre tying down a French Corps and so preventing it from joining Napoleon the next day on the main battlefield. He seemed to think he had missed out on the main action. Even the attempts in which he was involved in a junior capacity to reform the Prussian army were not entirely successful. They fell short of what he and others originally envisaged. And of course he died with his magnum opus incomplete and unpublished. But then the impossibility of all these hopes may have been essential to his commitment.

Clausewitz the Warrior

Clausewitz went into action for the first time a few days after his thirteenth birthday when his regiment stormed the village of Zahlbach and engaged in hand to hand combat. In the following weeks he was frequently under fire, and on one occasion barely escaped an ambush.

Clausewitz gives us an insight into the battle in the famous passage in which he makes much of the cannon balls whizzing overhead; the 'thunder of the guns'; the 'rattling of grapeshot on roofs'; and the 'air filled with hissing bullets' (*On War* 1, 13). This description of battle, of course, seems to us terribly dated, with its mention of rolling cannon balls and cavalry charges. Almost as dated, one might add, as descriptions of the 82nd Airborne Division or the 9th Infantry hitting the beaches of Normandy in 1944, wading through freezing water and hunkering down behind anti-tank obstacles, struggling against the ebb and flow of the tides. Our idea of combat is formed by the Second Battle of Fallujah (2005) during which the US Marines made their way through the city street by street and house by house under constant fire from rooftops, and in constant danger from planted explosives and booby traps. But the experience of battle is much the same: the confusion, the noise, the fear etched in Clausewitz's description, is to be found in every description of war.

The point is that Clausewitz probably felt most at home not in the classroom, but on the battlefield. There is a revealing passage in a letter he wrote to his then fiancée:

> My Fatherland needs the war, and frankly speaking, only war can bring me happiness. In whichever way I might like to relate my life to the rest of the world, my way takes me always across a great battlefield; unless I enter upon it, no permanent happiness can be mine. (Rapoport, 1982, 22)

The quotation offers us a window into Clausewitz's soul. It shows us the core of the man. To better grasp that fact let me quote a passage from Ralph Waldo Emerson's *Journals*:

> It is the largest part of a man that is not inventoried. He is many innumerable parts: he is social, professional, political, sectarian, literary, and of this or that set and corporation. But after the most exhausting census has been made, there remains as much more which no tongue can tell. And this remainder is that which interests. This is that which the preacher and the poet and the musicians speak of. This is that which the strong genius works upon; the region of destiny, of aspiration, of the unknown. ...

> For the best part, I repeat, of any mind is not that which he knows, but that which hovers in gleams, suggestions, tantalising unpossessed before him. His firm recorded knowledge soon loses all interest for him. But this dancing chorus of thoughts and hopes is the quarry of his future, is his possibility, and teaches him that his man's life is of a ridiculous brevity and meanness, but that it is his first age and trial only of his young wings ... (Bloom, 2015, 156–157)

It is a lengthy quote, but I think an illuminating one for those who agree with Emerson that creative writing and creative reading are interlinked. It affords us an insight into the daemonic nature of the man whose life we are trying to nail down. It is clear that Clausewitz loved war, much to the embarrassment of our age, but not his own. Soldiers these days are not encouraged to tell us that they love war; like oncologists they are expected to treat the symptoms of the disease, not compound them.

Unfortunately, Clausewitz was more interested in explaining his excitement rather than understanding the emotional currents that provoked it. If you take a book like Gerald Linderman's *The World Within War*, we find a much more profound understanding of the range of combat experience (Linderman, 1997). Linderman documents the kaleidoscope of emotions and feelings that men encounter in their first combat experience—the development of reflex actions and animal instincts; their nagging concerns about their own performance; their sense of excitement and fear and awareness of vulnerability. Combat alters a fighting man's sense of time, and tends to merge past and future with the present. This, for Linderman, is exactly 'the world within war' (Linderman, 1997). It would have been interesting had Clausewitz been more introspective than he was, but then we live in an age when psychological insight is everything and in which all experience is highly personalised. Clausewitz's age was much more guarded and officers were neither encouraged nor expected, to interrogate their emotional life too deeply.

Today, however, we know something Clausewitz didn't. Social psychologists tell us that people actually become what they do. Daryl Bem insists that people draw inferences about who they are by observing their own behaviour. It is called self-perception theory. On the day of his baptism of fire Clausewitz would have been prey to conflicting emotions. He would certainly have known fear; he had no idea how he would behave in the heat of battle. He tells us in his account of his first battlefield experience how soldiers notice how others behave around them. And that is what we now seize upon. Clearly, Bem noted, we have inner dispositions. Warriors, for example, really are 'born' and dispositions can indeed be partly 'trained in'. But we also act in ways we ourselves find strange because they are not always what we would have expected of ourselves. Tolstoy writes about this in *War and Peace* in the episode when Pierre finds himself at Borodino, to his intense surprise, helping Russian soldiers reload their guns. In going back and returning with the ammunition, he engages in a single, unreflective act of courage. As a result he experiences for the first time his own moral worth. In short, we are often unknown to ourselves. Introspection can help us only so much; our deeds—particularly in moments of crisis—ultimately define us. And our behaviour does not just reveal innate dispositions; from it we may even infer dispositions that were not there before.

Now, it is important to remember that soldiers in the heat of battle often behave bravely because they have no other choice; there is no line of retreat, no hiding from others. This is the message of Stephen Crane's novel, *The Red Badge of Courage*, which tells of a young man, trying his best to act the part and finding himself wanting. In the course of a day's battle, however, he eventually comes through. Only after the fact does he find that he is brave. And he is forced to become a hero because of social pressure (Crane, 1994). Warriors inhabit an intensely social world in which everyone counts on everyone else. Even in Clausewitz there may have been something of the actor. Clausewitz may have spent the next twenty years literally acting a part, 'faking it till you make it' to quote William James (Wilson, 2014, 54–5).

So Clausewitz's brief, less than one page, description of his feelings in battle has received scientific validation. It is only by observing ourselves that we know who we are. Strangest of all, wrote Philip Caputo in his Vietnam War memoir, 'was the sensation of watching myself in a movie… one part of course was doing something, while the other part watched from a distance.' (Caputo, 1999, 167). 'It was fucking cool', remarked one US Marine after a firefight in Iraq. It reminded him not of a movie, but of a game he played, *Grand Theft Auto:Vice City* (Wright, 2004, 5). And 'cool' is what Hollywood and the military-entertainment industry have made war for many young soldiers. The rap lyrics, and the gangsta-speak derived from movies, graphic novels and life on the street, are all reflective of a culture that still produces warriors who often only discover the fact by observing themselves in battle.

So was Clausewitz a Militarist?

'Too much Clausewitz', he went on. 'They're only interested in firepower.'

I have lifted this passage—a conversation between two scientists—from Fred Hoyle's classic 1964 work of science fiction, *The Black Cloud* (Hoyle, 2010, 175). It is a tale about an encounter with an alien race. And it was typical of the genre in the 1960s that whenever intelligent life in the solar system was discovered, the military set out to destroy it, much to the dismay of the scientists who made first contact.

Hollywood loves to depict generals as unthinking when confronted with aliens—instinctively distrusting, idiots in all but name (living up to the famous joke that military intelligence is an oxymoron). The film critic Damon Knight originally coined the term 'second-order idiot plot' to refer to a story that features a fictional group of people who could exist in real life only if everyone else is an idiot. It is a familiar theme in nuclear Armageddon movies in which those who are not idiots only get to find out who they are when it is too late to undo the damage (as in the case in Dr Strangelove [1963] and the TV mini-series, *Whoops Apocalypse* [1983–7]).

Clausewitz's own reputation therefore suffers simply because he was a military man, who seemed to have been in love with war. And if you are of a certain disposition then you are unlikely to warm to the man. There is plenty you can find fault with: idealism he tells us is no substitute for 'a thirst for fame or honour' (*On War*, 1, 3). At one point he talks of the 'effeminacy of feeling' that a long peace produces, and the 'degeneracy' that follows the naked pursuit of profit in the marketplace rather than quest for glory on a battlefield (On War, 3, 6). Such attitudes were common enough at the time and indeed for some time afterwards. Our forebears were not as sensitive as we are to other peoples' feelings. Take for example Lawrence of Arabia's remark that he was better qualified than any other professor to translate the *Iliad*—unlike most of them he had actually killed people (and a good many more I might add than the sixty-four heroes who are actually named by Homer in the twenty-four books of the epic poem) (Nicolson, 2014, 47).

I think what some of my students find particularly distressing about Clausewitz is his apparent lack of emotional engagement. Nietzsche tells us that our thoughts are shadows of our feelings—darker, emptier, and simpler. Clausewitz is often accused of being out of touch with his feelings or revealing too little about them. This is not entirely fair, of course; he tells us after all that he could never rid himself of the horrors he had witnessed at first hand as Napoleon's army attempted to cross the Berezina River during the retreat from Moscow. But he does say very little about the features of war that since 1914 we have found most important: fear, the killing, the trauma. The exploration of all of three are now considered essential to a moral education. This can be spontaneous (known as 'emotional mirroring') or more conscious or deliberate ('perspective taking'). But for all his interest in psychology Clausewitz's age didn't go in for emotional mirroring, and in the absence of neuroscience it didn't understand the importance of mirror neurons which explain why we feel distress when confronted with the horrors of war—in itself, of course, a kind of 'motor empathy' (Gerrans, 2015, 11).

So, was Clausewitz a militarist? Apart from the fact that the term was not coined until comparatively late in the day, the answer must be an emphatic no. A militarist is a man (always a man, by the way) who in believing that war counts for everything, counts for nothing himself. Clausewitz never laboured under any misapprehension of what war actually was—he had experienced it at first hand. He wrote his work precisely in order to explain why we must put limits to military action; why we must acknowledge that if war is indeed the continuation of politics, it is often a very imperfect political instrument. The debt we owe to him can only be repaid by reading him as we should. That debt is not so much in knowledge, but in understanding (our ability to think it through). And that is the main difference between his work and that of his contemporaries, including Antoine-Henri Jomini (who influenced both German and American thinking before 1914). It is a difference both of kind and degree, and that double difference continues to define the central importance of his lifetime's study.

Excursus—Where is the Post Traumatic Stress?

Combat has offered for centuries the highest production values of any form of human activity, and the Napoleonic Wars were no exception. But that is only one of the many faces of war. You won't find any reference in Clausewitz to combat fatigue (Post-Traumatic Stress Disorder), or mutiny (collective indiscipline), even though they are part of the landscape of every war. For Keegan, Clausewitz was deficient in the emotional register of his work: where is the human suffering and the darker side of war, the looting and the rapes and the mind-numbing boredom?

It is dangerous, however, to ascribe to people of the past one's own emotions. Why should the past reflect back our own image of ourselves? Why should the soldiers of Clausewitz's time project back models of our own concerns and behaviour? Fast-back to the ancient world where, Jason Crowley reminds us, soldiers of the day entered combat with a historically specific set of norms and values and fought in a historically specific environment (Crowley, 2014). Edith Hall insists that the citizens of the Greek city-states understood the simplicity, clarity and brevity of battle, which determined their entire relationship with their own family as well as community. They took pride in the death of their enemies as well as pride in their own personal tally of kills (Hall, 2014, 174). A famous epitaph from Megara in Ancient Greece records that the celebrated warrior descended to the Underworld 'having brought sorrow to no-one on earth'. Nothing more demonstrates that the sorrow of his enemies—their grieving families and orphaned children—was not merely inconsequential, but actually beyond reflective consideration. Killing was not, in other words, 'psychologically toxic', but expected (Crowley, 2014, 117). From this we might deduce that post-traumatic stress was not a major problem in the ancient world, which is why the sources never mention it. Sometimes absence of evidence is indeed evidence of absence.

In Clausewitz's day battles did not last for weeks or months, but only for a day or two at most. And for every one who is scarred by war others remain remarkably untouched by it. All one can posit is that the military culture of early nineteenth century Europe was very different from our own. War was part of its *Lebenswelt* (or 'life-world') and there was no problem for the re-socialisation of men returning home to civilian life (the real challenge was poverty). In a word, the gap between the two worlds—the civilian and military—was not as great as it is today. Keegan puts it thus in his *A History of Warfare:* 'War is fought by warriors from a very ancient world which exists in parallel with our everyday world but does not belong to it. Both worlds evolve over time; both adapt, but the warrior world follows the civilian at a distance, and the distance can never be closed.' (Keegan, 1993, xvi).

Today the distance is much greater than it has ever been. We now have to deal with the challenge of what Frank Furedi calls 'emotional determinism'. The state of our emotions is represented very often as the cause of all problems, including PTSD. War itself is represented as a traumatic break from the norms of civilian life and soldiers are seen as inevitable victims. The ethic of suffering has replaced the ethic of achievement as the dominant 'intellectual moral truth' of war itself

(Furedi, 2004, 11). It is an ethical minefield, of course. For those who claim that trauma is now an epidemic in Western militaries, there are also those who argue that anti-war psychiatrists exploit gullible young men for their own political purposes and unnecessarily invalidise them. Many psychiatrists who have worked in non-Western cultures see PTSD as a piece of American cultural imperialism—the 'Coca-Cola of psychiatry', according to the German psychiatrist David Becker. Whether PTSD is a condition determined by biology or is shaped by culture is a question that admits to no final answer. My suspicion is that medical theorists such as Derek Somerfield and Allan Young are probably right in arguing that it is not timeless and has evolved in response to cultural conditioning (Shephard, 2015, 7). Indeed, the fact that Clausewitz does not mention it may be the most interesting evidence of all.

What makes Clausewitz modern?

Ultimately we read Clausewitz's work because he is modern; he is one of us. Students often beg to disagree. And we can see where they are coming from. Prussia, after all, was not especially modern in 1792. It was a poor and impoverished kingdom, out of left field, one might say, of the Enlightenment, though it could claim such intellectual giants as Immanuel Kant and Hegel. It had not yet industrialised and was not to do so for some time. We will discuss Clausewitz's attitude to technology separately, but the greatest dissimilarity between our age and his own is not so much the absence of factory organisation and coal-powered machinery, but the absence of the most important innovation of all—what the philosopher Alfred Whitehead called 'the invention of the method of invention.'

Even so, many of Clausewitz's preoccupations are similar to our own. Let me mention just three.

The first and perhaps most important is that Clausewitz lived in an age of Enlightenment, in the shadow of which we still live. Clausewitz is often called a counter-Enlightenment thinker, but this is deeply misleading. True, he espoused the German Romantic belief in psychological thinking as opposed to the cold, calculating reason of the French *philosophes*. But like his inspiration Kant, Clausewitz believed that man is an autonomous moral agent. This 'science of man' produced what

Vincenzo Ferrone in his history of the Enlightenment calls an 'episte-mological revolution' which gave rise in turn to a modern sensibility (Ferrone, 2015). History now had a narrative—that of Christian tele-ology stripped of its theology—the progression of Man (the march to a more perfect society). And this also meant for Clausewitz the march towards a more perfect form of war based on the Enlightenment's faith in education. Clausewitz's regimental commander founded a school in the 1790s for Non-Commissoned Officers. He wanted the common soldier to take part in Kant's *Aufklarung* ('enlightened age') and believed that the primary function of education was not the acquisition of knowledge but the cultivation of judgment. The same aim is to be found in Goerg Heinrich von Berenhorst's *Reflections on the Art of War* (1798), which was highly influential in Clausewitz's lifetime even if it is now totally forgotten (Harari, 2008, 168).

The problem was that no one could agree on the goal of history. Kant identified the age with the enlightened despotism of Frederick the Great; Hegel with the mystical unfurling of Absolute Spirit which found its instantiation briefly in the figure of Napoleon. If two Prussian Lutherans could not agree the rest of Europe had no chance. The French Revolution only added to the confusion: did it owe more to the price of bread than the ideas of Rousseau, who wanted to force people to be free? Hegel called the state the vehicle for the human spirit; but if Napoleon was the revolution's dialectical outcome did the future promise freedom or tyranny? No-one could say for sure. This ambiva-lence can be found in Clausewitz's understanding of war: could war be perfected, or would it end in even greater violence, relatively uncon-strained by politics or reason? Clausewitz glimpsed the future—just once, in Book 8, Chapter 6B. The Europeans of his day had observed limits that stopped war from becoming total thanks only to 'an uncon-sciousness of what is possible.' What would happen if they ever grasped the possibilities that lay hidden?

There is a second strand in Clausewitz's thinking that makes him a thoroughly modern figure: his obsession with 'efficiency.' It is one of the big ideas that has shaped the modern world. His great mentor Scharnhorst told his students at the Military Academy that survival in the modern age demanded efficiency in exploiting the physical and social resources at the disposal of the state (Lebow, 2003, 179). What

Clausewitz found most powerful in revolutionary France's view of war was the *Levée en masse* (conscription)—the mobilisation of human/social capital. What we find central to his admiration for Napoleon is the efficient use of military power, the concentration of force. Clausewitz's impulse was always to look for the driving energy behind war, whether in the form of intellect (in the case of Frederick the Great) or will (in the case of Napoleon). Charles Tilly perhaps puts it best:

> Over the last thousand years European states have undergone a peculiar evolution: from wasps to locomotives. Long they concentrated on war, leaving most activities to other organisations just as long as those organisations yielded tribute at appropriate intervals. Tribute-taking states remained fierce but light in weight by comparison with their bully successors; they stung but they did not suck dry. As time went on states—even the capital intensive varieties—took on activities, powers and commitments whose very support constrained them. These locomotives ran on the rails of sustenance for the civilian population and maintenance by a civilian staff. Off the rails, the warlike engines could not run at all. (Tilly, 1992, 96)

This development was asymmetrical in that efficiency growth in one sector was not always matched in another. But Clausewitz's entire project was driven by the need to make the conduct of war more efficient at achieving political and limited goals. And what he is really offering his readers is what we would now call know-how.

To be sure, historians ever since have spent a lot of time reminding us that Napoleon could only conscript a relatively small percentage of the French population (the army with which he marched to Moscow was largely made up of mercenaries and foreign contingents supplied by his allies). The state was not quite the bureaucratic behemoth it was later to become. National consciousness, certainly in Prussia, was relatively unformed and many of the reforms that the Prussian Army undertook after 1806 were undone in the peace that followed. But what we take to be a modern way of war is one that is represented by the investment by the state in human and social capital; in constant innovation and inventiveness; and in bureaucratic controls including the statistical modelling of society that was shortly to follow. Even Clausewitz's career was distinctively 'modern.' Van Creveld criticises him for saying little about staff organisation and logistics, which he reminds us is so central to waging war today, though Clausewitz was principally a staff officer, a representative if you like of the new 'professional class' that only really came into its own after his death, but which helped win Prussia its war against France in 1870.

Let me mention a third reason why Clausewitz can be considered a thoroughly modern author: the importance he attached to his own age. We moderns are inveterately 'presentist'—we privilege our own times even though we know in our hearts it is three-dimensional: the present is influenced by the future as much as the past. One way to grasp this is through literature. Think of an early eighteenth century work by the Enlightenment philosopher Diderot. The hero of his tale *Jacques the Fatalist* joins a regiment and is seriously wounded in battle. Marked for life, he will limp for the rest of his days. But what war has he fought in, and what battle? Diderot does not bother to tell us. It was only with the Napoleonic Wars that novelists like Balzac and Scott began to make clear which wars they are describing in their fiction. Characters like Stendhal's Fabricio, who fights at Waterloo, live in precisely dated times; they are usually acutely aware of the significance of their era. Clausewitz too believed his service in 1792 had been of historic importance: 'My entrance into the world occurred at the scene of great events where the destiny of nations was decided', he wrote to his future wife (Stoker, 2014, 9).

Clausewitz, in short, was intensely conscious of living through a critical and significant point in history. What makes his 'take' on the revolutionary wars so important is that he thought they represented a case of energetic transformation in which an entire people took part in sustaining a conflict which they did not know how to end except with the complete destruction of the enemy, even at the risk of bringing about their own. The Napoleonic era was not one of total war, though it was perhaps the nearest Europe came to it before 1914. War intruded into economic life and social experience as it rarely had before. Clausewitz also tended to give it a historical life of its own, although it was rooted in the history of pre-revolutionary Europe. The point is that it also gave rise to one of the most stable periods of European history, a long peace which eluded the belligerents after 1918. Even when the 1848 revolutions broke out they failed to catch fire; as A. J. P. Taylor put it, 1848 was a turning point that failed to turn.

Even so, it is thanks in part to the spin that Clausewitz gave it that we tend to see the period 1792–1815 as the birth of 'modern' warfare.

One doesn't have to be a card-carrying Hegelian, writes Robert Pippin, to believe that modernity had very distinctive credentials: the idea of novelty for its own sake; the radical escape from tradition; the dream of revolutionary change. All three suggested the extent of the historical rupture. Clausewitz's great inspiration, as we shall see, was Kant, and for Pippin it is Kant who in *The Critique of Pure Reason* inaugurated the modern idea of a new self-determining beginning. 'His project is more consistent than any other with modernity's general understanding as an origination in history, a beginning not bounded or conditioned by tradition or religious authority, finally free and independent, and so fully self-conscious about its own possibility.' (Pippin, 2003, 46). The same might also be said of the implicit message of Clausewitz's book, *On War*.

Clausewitz's precursors

Every great author has his precursors, even if sometimes the very pervasiveness of an influence makes it difficult to trace. We are not ourselves until we know how little of ourselves is truly our own. 'Great men are more distinguished by range and extent than by originality— the greatest genius is the most indebted man.' (Bate, 2008, 133). Emerson's point is well taken. It is often difficult to see just how deeply an influence penetrates to make possible a great, original mind. But as Emerson went on to add, originality is also the product of circumstances. You don't set out to write a great work; you find yourself 'in the river of thoughts and events forced onward by the ideas and necessities of [your] contemporaries' (Bate, 2008, 152). Hence the importance of the Napoleonic wars, in just the same way that Sun Tzu was influenced by the period of the Warring Kingdoms in China and Thucydides by the Peloponnesian war, the most destructive conflict in the ancient Greek world.

Still, it is always difficult to trace the influences on any writer because they are not always aware of them themselves. Some of the principal precepts in Clausewitz's work can be found in a very ancient source, the *De Re Militari* by Flavius Vegetius. Vegetius' book was very popular in the mediaeval world. Among his key concepts was the importance of strategic reserves. In business strategy, writes Stephen Morillo, this concept has morphed into what we call 'emergent strategy'. Business strategists like Henry Mintzberg insist that over-planning leads to the investment of resources and initiatives that may not work. Comparing typical strategic planning to 'programming', Mintzberg suggests that we should view the strategist as an experimenter: he tries several things, sees what works, then follows up with a deployment of reserves in the form of reserve capital and available personnel, aimed precisely at the point of weakness duly uncovered. The strategic use of reserves is in many ways the essence of what a business strategy is all about. Once called 'the art and science of options', strategy as a domain of thought is epitomised by the notion of keeping one's options open so that the best possible solution is available at just the right time (Morillo).

Another major source of Clausewitz's thinking may have been Machiavelli's *Art of War*, to which he referred in a letter to the philosopher Fichte (1809). Until Clausewitz's own work established itself in military academies, *The Art of War* was read more widely than any other military text, and it is taken by some critics to mark the birth of modern military thought. One writer concludes that in its emphasis on a people in arms, the ideal of a decisive victory; the undertaking of war as a continuation of politics by other means; and the importance of concentrating one's forces at a critical point, Machiavelli's thinking can be considered thoroughly 'Clausewitzian' (Lynch, 2003, xxix). Can we agree in the end with Borges that a great author creates his own precursors?

One can press home the point even further: Machiavelli and Clausewitz shared a similar aim, namely to restore excellence to the conduct of war. In the case of the former the model was Rome at the height of its power. *The Art of War* is the expression of a unique Renaissance confidence in the possibility of a synthesis of ancient and modern, a perfect example of the revaluation of a tradition in an early modern context. In the case of Clausewitz the Napoleonic model of war was the supreme expression of excellence, too.

Several other influences can also be identified. Take Clausewitz's brief discussion of the origin of war; it dates back, he tells us, to when a defender first hits back, when two or more people hit upon the idea of organised resistance. Where did he get this idea from? Perhaps from one of his favourite philosophers, Montesquieu, who wrote, that 'once in a political society men lose their feeling of weakness whereupon their former equality disappears and the state of war begins.' It is a brilliant observation: the state and the state of war come into existence at much the same time. It is a variation of Charles Tilly's famous formula that war made the state and the state made war. It is a paradox: states provide the in-group with security only at the cost of permanent insecurity against the out-group. William Bryce Gallie's own formulation is better: irrespective of their origins, war and the state have developed under similar competitive conditions (Gallie, 1991, 31). What he finds particularly surprising is that while political philosophers spent centuries analysing the state—beginning with Plato and *The Republic*—few bothered to subject war to any sustained analysis. But his explanation is convincing. War defies theorising, doesn't it? It is contingent, brutal and often incomprehensible. It is also, of course, inescapable, so what is the point of thinking about it?

Ultimately, what makes *On War* so remarkable is not the assimilation of other authors but the very scope of its ambition. Like Vico's *New Science* (which is little read these days except by academics) the greatness of Clausewitz's work is to be measured by the tasks its author set himself. In the case of both the tasks were so original that they and their first readers were not even aware of their originality (Gallie, 1991, 39). Thus Vico thought he had written another book on jurisprudence when in fact he had invented the philosophy of history. Vico, it has been claimed, thought like a 'depth psychologist' (Hillsman, 2004, 7). He sought to strip away Enlightenment rationality and plumb the depths: to uncover the mythic, poetic and archetypal patterns of the imagination. In Clausewitz's case he probably only set out to write a manual for senior officers and found to his surprise that he had ended up producing the very first phenomenology of war.

Clausewitz: Phenomenologist

In invoking the term I am not referring to the philosophical school which includes amongst its first practitioner, Edmund Husserl (1859–1938). Peter Paret believes that Clausewitz's approach to knowledge was akin to that of Husserlian phenomenology in that he believed it possible to make definitions about the essence of war which derived from pure analytical thought rather than inductive generalisation

(Paret, 2007, 357). It is an interesting idea, but not one I want to run with, not least because this book is written for students of war, not students of philosophy, and it is probably best for the former to give Husserl a wide berth.

Let us stick with what the dictionary tells us: a phenomenology is principally a style of enquiry. The Greek word *phainomenon* is the science of that which appears to be true. We must try to get behind appearances, to the essence of the subject in question. It was the French historian Marc Bloch who wrote that our intelligence is stimulated not by the wish to know but the wish to understand the relationship between phenomena. Of course knowledge must be real knowledge and understanding must accompany it from the beginning. The fundamental thrust of Clausewitz's enquiry was to comprehend the relationship between politics and war. For that reason it has often been said that 'Politics and War' might have been a better title for his book.

Clausewitz was not a philosopher, but he lived at a time when professional philosophers were about to hijack thinking, as well as the business of thinking about thinking, and to do so in a language largely inaccessible to all but philosophers themselves. Today Anglo-American philosophers still prefer it when nothing is discussed except the means of discussion. Clausewitz would have been very critical of this because of his strongly held belief that reason has a need to actualise itself in action; politicians should think and so should soldiers, and not allow their thinking to be done by others.

But if Clausewitz was not a philosopher, then exactly what was he? He was not a professional historian, I think we can agree, because of his tendency at times to over-subordinate evidence to interpretation, and he was certainly not a political scientist (indeed he was not as well-versed in political thought as he might have been). Although he claimed that war was a product of social life he was not really a social theorist let alone a sociologist (Comte only coined the term seven years after his death).

Clausewitz's greatest interpreter Raymond Aron came up with another formulation: he called him a 'theologian of war' because he questioned the persistence of war no more than theologians question the existence of God (Aron, 1976/83, ix). But that actually is a bit of a cop-out because there are two ways of understanding theological knowledge. One is theological naturalism, in which reason leads to belief, or the propositions of faith are derived from human experience. The other is theological positivism in which faith is accepted on a voluntary basis, that is, reasoning takes place within faith, rather than as a basis for it. It is not altogether clear which side of the argument Clausewitz would have been on. He doesn't tell us whether he reasons out the resilience of war from history or human nature or whether Augustine was right to see it as evidence of the inherent sinfulness of the human condition (which means that even those engaged in a just war cannot escape from its contaminating influence), or whether in Kantian terms it is evidence of free will—God grants us the right to kill each other in order to discern our moral development, or lack of it over time. For that reason I think Gallie was right to call Clausewitz a phenomenologist.

Now, any phenomenological investigation worth its salt should try to uncover the invariant structures of the phenomenon in question; it should try to bring to light what William Hewell called 'a consilience of inductions' (academic-speak for a convergence of evidence). Thus Evolution as a theory is only as strongly entrenched as it is thanks to support from an ever-greater number of sub-fields: geology, palaeontology, biology, herpetology, entomology, bio-geography, physiology and comparative anatomy. Each scientist works in his own field but if he is up to the job tries to be aware of research in others. Progress in one usually is accompanied by progress in another—in short, by a 'consilience of inductions'. And to postulate, as Clausewitz does, that war has a nature which requires evidence from a multiplicity of sources: from anthropology, philosophy, physics, sociology, economics, history, as well as from literature.

There is a lot missing because he had no access to the tools of understanding we have. As Gallie insists, for that reason alone his theory is incomplete (Gallie, 1991, 62). He offers us a phenomenology of war without, for example, telling us much about its physiology—the vital forces that call it out and keep it going. Unlike us he didn't have access to the behavioural sciences or evolutionary psychology. Gallie maintains that if Clausewitz had lived later he might have chosen to cast his ideas within some kind of evolutionary framework in which every important war would play the role of a variation which helps to decide the future life-forms of war. Unfortunately he died almost forty years before Darwin put pen to paper, a point I will discuss at length in Chapter 3.

And he was also writing, of course, long before Freud. Although he did invoke psychology (the 'art bablative' his contemporary the poet Southey scornfully called it), he did not share Freud's belief that it inheres in the social-psychological tension that exists between different drives and pressures. He did not see it as a primordial force of instinctual aggression, though one writer, Daniel Pick, thinks that his definition of war as a 'pulsation of violence' is pretty suggestive of the male sexual drive (Pick, 1993, 35). The 'sexualisation of war' had to await the atomic age. Carol Cohn reports on a university course on defence technology which she found to be heavily sexualised with lectures on 'vertical erector launches', 'thrust-to-weight ratios', 'soft lay-downs', 'deep penetration' and endless discussions about the comparative advantage of a protracted nuclear strike as opposed to a short, sharp sudden attack, or what one adviser to the National Security Council called the possibility of 'releasing 80 per cent of our mega-tonnage in one orgasmic whump.' (Cohn, 2004)

Since Clausewitz's day the phenomenological approach has expanded greatly thanks to studies such as social psychology and even neuroscience. There is even a new 'science' called neuro-marketing which uses brain scans to uncover the mental triggers that determine what we purchase. *Forbes* hails it as a 'great milestone in business' thinking (Carr, 2008, 267). Models using psychology, though not yet to my knowledge neuroscience, are being employed to investigate the neural pathways of the financial traders who brought us the crash of 2008. It is a beginning, though the interest shown in the studies by the traders themselves is unlikely to be great. But if we really can measure the ecstatic vision of nuns through FMRI scans, couldn't we do the same with Jihadists in the Greater Middle East?

Objective

Students continue to see Clausewitz as embodying the importance of studying war in a classroom but the subject embodies its own seriousness or it would never have been worth studying in the first place. Anyway my aim in writing this book is to bring Clausewitz to life for a modern student audience largely through scripts of the great man's invented conversations with modern Anglo-American audiences. I intersperse these sections with chapters which locate Clausewitz in his times for unlike Schopenhauer, a near contemporary, he was not a man who educated himself against the age (the phrase is Nietzsche's); he was very much in tune with it, while transcending it at the same time.

It is worthwhile for that reason to consider how he might have dealt with some of our own strategic challenges (the subject of Chapter 4) which I hope in turn will show that *On War* and many of his essays are still relevant and illuminating. The fictional interludes also allow me to critique some contemporary fads by showing that some are rooted in old fallacies. I hope to challenge a view that was fashionable in the 1990s that his work had reached its sell-by date in an age of 'new wars' and non-state actors. We were often told that the latest Revolution in Military Affairs (RMA) had consigned his magnum opus to the scrap-heap; that the 'fog of war' had been dispelled and 'friction' diminished. Since 2001 a new generation of scholars has kicked back and I am deeply indebted to their work.

Rebooting Clausewitz departs notably, however, from the scholarly approach traditional among scholars of the great man. It's tone sits uneasily with the reverence usually paid his work. This book is written for students who like a challenge; it engages them in a language that they might find more appealing because it breaks with convention. Let me be the first to acknowledge that this approach has problems of its own; my interrogators in the fictional interludes speak in long sentences and with a degree of fluency that we usually don't encounter in everyday conversation. My West Point instructor is unusually well-read. And Clausewitz himself speaks in cadences that would not have been his own. As for what he himself would have made of this book: well, that is a question probably best left unasked.

2

CLAUSEWITZ AT WEST POINT

It is 4 o'clock on a dark Wednesday evening in November. Autumn is surrendering to its end with a sort of melancholy resignation. Fifteen cadets are taking an exam on the theory of war later in the week. On War *is one of the set texts. The Instructor ruminates on what they will make of their guest—the German writer, Carl von Clausewitz who has just entered the seminar room. He is a visiting Fellow of the Academy this year. And he has already created a stir by voicing his disdain for modern military life—the specialised* argot *of war which he claims to find incomprehensible; the general demeanour of the cadets (though he likes the Prussian crew cuts). Jousting with especially outspoken female cadets is clearly an ordeal for him. But he is nothing if not polite. He is learning quickly. He is adapting to twenty-first century military life. Today is his last appearance in a classroom before he returns home. Where will he go with this? the Colonel wonders. How does he compare our young men (and women) with the students of his own Academy in Berlin? Will either engage with each other this afternoon?*

INSTRUCTOR: We're really privileged, ladies and gentlemen, to have with us today the author of perhaps the most important book ever written on our subject of study at the Academy. It is one of the ten military classics on our syllabus. You know him principally as an author but he is also a fine solider, an astute staff officer, one might even say the founding father of the theory of war.

CLAUSEWITZ: Well, after an introduction like that I can hardly wait to hear what I am going to say. (Laughter) Yet I find that in all the airport bookshops it's Sun Tzu and not me who seems to sell. When I first arrived in your country I saw a book at the airport called *The Art of War for Dating: Master Sun Tzu's Tactics to Win Over Women*. I don't think my book is going to help you with that challenge. (Laughter) And don't think I am not aware that at the Army War College the joke is that reading my work is the best cure for insomnia!

INSTRUCTOR: Well, cadets, you can see that the general has a fine sense of humour. And I agree with him; when Paris Hilton is photographed with a copy of Sun Tzu's book perhaps it really is time to call time on the *Art of War*.

But let us turn to the substantive discussion. As you will see from the Power Points I have put up on the screen, we are going to divide this seminar into four sessions.

Slide One

WORKSHOP ON THE THEORY OF WAR

Critical Workshop Questions

- What is Theory?
- Why do Theory?
- How to do Theory?
- What has Theory achieved?

INSTRUCTOR: So let us begin at the beginning.

Slide Two

WHAT IS THEORY?

- What is the relationship of Theory to Practice?
- How does Theory differ from other similar inquiries such as philosophy and history?
- Is Theory an art or a science?

CLAUSEWITZ: Well, before I begin, can I say that I am a little surprised to find that you are reading my book. It was never intended for anyone but Staff officers or those in high command; I never expected it to be carried onto a battlefield (*On War, 2, 2*). I will repeat what I said: my book is simply too complex for young people. It is even difficult for generals, especially American generals I might add, who think they are devotees of my ideas but have a very imperfect understanding of them. And when you're under fire you really are on your own—you have to rely on your own intuition and imagination, neither of which can be taught in a classroom.

INSTRUCTOR: Point taken, General. I understand where you are coming from. But you know you are partly responsible for why we get our young men and women to theorise early in their careers. In your day a theory meant coming up with a formula or an established procedure of doing things. You redefined it to mean a framework of study. In doing so you really did revolutionise military thinking, more so perhaps than you yourself recognised at the time (Echevarria, 1995, 6). And this is why we get the cadets to read your work even if it is difficult to understand at first reading.

CADET 1: Are you saying, Sir, that theories of war are of limited value?

CLAUSEWITZ: I'm not saying that at all, young man. Remember there are two kinds of theory. The first allows us to reproduce the particular phenomenon we are studying by collecting data and analysing it. The other approach is to analyse the phenomenon you are studying in the abstract and tease out some patterns that you find reappearing over time.

Let me give you an example. One of the great puzzles in war is that when you start to kill one another, chaos should ensue: passions are ignited; vengeance becomes an imperative of its own. But in fact, chaos doesn't usually result. War usually has some kind of structure—a beginning and an end. It may have a tendency to escape control entirely but it usually doesn't. There is a controlling will: politics. Societies don't fight to the last man; many even come to terms with their defeat. They get over it very quickly.

INSTRUCTOR: Occasionally they may even embrace it. *Embracing Defeat* is the title of a book on post-war Japan by one of our historians, John Dower. You could write a book with the same title about post-war Germany but not alas, post-Cold War Russia.

But may we move on? What makes your work challenging, I think, is that you were the first writer to apply science, philosophy and history to an understanding of war.

CLAUSEWITZ: Since we have started with science let me say something more about it. Remember, people often think that scientists discover things by chance. They usually don't. Most scientists don't observe nature, so much as interrogate it with a hypothesis that they have already formulated. In other words they know what to look for. They then devise tests to confirm their hypothesis and examine the data to see whether it holds up. Scientific work is really about what to observe, how to observe it, and how to test what one is observing.

I formulated a hypothesis—well several, in fact. Let me mention just one—war has a tendency to escalate. It was a hypothesis based on induction (the evidence of history), which allowed me in turn to make a deduction (a specific prediction about a probability that inheres in war itself). But that deduction of course falls far short of being a scientific law.

I think we can agree that science compels belief, social theory doesn't. Thanks to empirical observation and mathematical proofs scientists can force agreement. Social theorists rely on argument alone. Scientists also can prove their hypotheses are true thanks to controlled experiments and mathematical axioms. And although mathematical axioms are often employed in philosophy, they are used differently—instead of compelling belief, more often than not they leave questions begging. Let me try to put it as simply as I can. Scientific theories change only when our knowledge of the world changes; non-scientific theories change all the time.

INSTRUCTOR: Let me remind the cadets that science deals with Level 1 chaotic systems like the weather. Social science deals with Level 2 chaotic systems like history. In the case of the weather we can accurately predict whether it will rain or not within say a 48-hour period. We can even engage in longer term predictions with a degree of confidence if we have the right computer models. But predictions never work in history because once you make a prediction history changes. What would happen if you could design a computer program that could predict the price of oil over the next ten years with 100 per cent accuracy? The price would immediately react to the forecast, which is why the forecast would prove wrong (Harari, 2014, 267–268).

CLAUSEWITZ: There is a larger point here.

No scientific theory can change what a theory is about. Newton's law of universal gravitation, for example, did not change the laws of gravity. But a theory of war can change the way war is waged. Physics is symmetrical, war is not. That is to say that the same basic features of a phenomenon are unchanging in the face of changing points of view. If we stand at the base of a house then look at it from above, it will look very different. But the laws that govern the construction of the building—straight lines and right angles in the same plane—remain untouched. That is not true of war which is asymmetrical; everything can change from the point of view of those who conduct it.

INSTRUCTOR: Could you tell the students a little more about how your study of philosophy influenced your theory of war?

CLAUSEWITZ: I know that military men, and today women too (you must excuse my occasional lapse on this point! I am suffering from historical jetlag), often find philosophical theories particularly abstruse. It's an old belief that philosophers and generals don't mix. You probably don't know the story of Hannibal and his encounter with Phormio, who was the most renowned philosopher of his day. The story goes that when he was living in exile in Ephesus he was invited to attend a lecture by the philosopher on the nature of battle command. It went down well with everyone in the audience except Hannibal himself who candidly remarked that the philosopher should have stuck to a subject about which he was well informed. Excusing himself as a Carthaginian whose understanding of Greek was imperfect, he then stuck in the knife: he had seen many doddering old men in his time but never anyone more senile than Phormio. I, too, have seen many doddering old men in my time, but they have been generals, not philosophers. (Laughter)

Anyway, my thinking owes a lot to the most important philosopher of my day, Immanuel Kant. By the way, I was taught by a Kantian scholar, Johan Gottfried Karl Christian Kiesewetter when I first began my studies at the Military Academy in 1801.

INSTRUCTOR: Might I even suggest that you could have called your book 'A Critique of War' after Kant's *Critique of Pure Reason*.

CLAUSEWITZ: Perhaps. Certainly in the Kantian sense of the word— a demystifying of a phenomenon in terms of that which we think of as a given. Kant was trying to penetrate to the reality behind appearance: the difference between the noumenal and phenomenal worlds. It is an endeavour in philosophy that dates back to Plato. Every culture produces a screen to facilitate its behaviour. Everything is ultimately dependent on the imagination. As you know I was critical of the 'cabinet wars' of the eighteenth century in which states had fought with one arm tied behind their backs. War is what we care to make of it and in Napoleon I recognised someone who thought about war more imaginatively than his predecessors, a general who unlocked its possibilities by penetrating to its core. And Kant was important to me on another count. I was interested in the rational control of war and in the *Critique of Pure Reason* Kant had probed the very limitations of rationality itself.

INSTRUCTOR: Can I ask you to probe a little more deeply?

CLAUSEWITZ: My thinking can be considered to be Kantian in at least three other respects. The first is the extent to which I engage in abstraction. Kant was interested in commonalities, not individual differences. He liked to find what things have in common, and to uncover their universal quality or essence. I suppose essentialising is what philosophers have been doing ever since the Greeks told us that what made us human is the use of reason. For me the essence of war is violence. 'War is an act of violence to compel an enemy to do our will.' That is only one definition I came up with. Here is another: 'War is a clash between major interests which is resolved by bloodshed. It is the only way in which it differs from other concepts.'

Point Two. Kant argued that the world is apprehended through intellectual concepts. You can take an individual thing—say a society—and consider it as a thing in itself. You can analyse its size, its constitutional composition, its value and belief systems, its moral and social norms. That is what Montesquieu, another philosopher who influenced me a lot, accomplished in his famous book, *The Spirit of the Laws*. So, I felt particularly confident in making the bold claim that war is 'the province of social life' precisely because it is determined by the size of a society, its constitution, its political and social character and the beliefs of its people. It is also important to understand the stories it tells itself. What are its prevailing narratives? If like the French you publish the Declaration of the Rights of Man (1789) you may find yourself fighting to liberate mankind from tyranny as the French revolutionary armies claimed. And you can compare and contrast one society with another using precisely the same categories.

INSTRUCTOR: Also you owe to Kant, I think, your insistence that there is a difference between practical and pure reason.

CLAUSEWITZ: Absolutely. The primary purpose of any theory is to help us to be more successful in the world of action (*On War*, 2, 1). Practical reason is what it says it is; we apply reason to think out what we should do in any particular situation. Pure reason allows us to escape from our immediate circumstances and discover certain trends or logical consistencies that transcend time and culture. Kant tells us that human beings are essentially beings who think necessarily in terms of logical forms. Pure reason is the attempt to know the world 'as it is' free from any conditions to which it

CLAUSEWITZ AT WEST POINT

may be subject such as the outside factors that govern our day to day thinking. Pure reason aims to view the world from no particular point of view. It is distinguished by the fact that it tries to make judgements of its own using ideas from which all empirical conditions have been removed (Scruton et al, 1997, 53–54). We can then abstract certain laws, or principles, or rules of life, that enable us to operate in the real world.

CADET 2: So this is how you came to the conclusion that war has its own logic, one that the human mind can reason out: it has a tendency to escalate. Limited wars are always in danger of becoming 'absolute.'

CADET 2: Yeah, that's a point that Denzel Washington makes in the movie *Crimson Tide*. Gene Hackman, who plays the captain of a nuclear submarine, asks his Executive Officer whether it was a mistake to bomb Hiroshima. He refers to you by name, General, though not very flatteringly I am afraid. In my day, he remarks, naval officers were expected to study physics, not the work of a nineteenth century philosopher. Washington replies that all that Clausewitz—I mean you, Sir—was trying to say is that the purpose of war is to serve a political end but that the true nature of war is to serve its own ends. In a nuclear world the true enemy would be war itself.

CLAUSEWITZ: I can't say I've seen the film; but it sounds as though the officer was asking the right questions.

CADET 2: But here's the thing, Sir. We know reality to be infinitely more complex than you did at the time you were writing your book. Social psychologists tell us about confirmation bias and cognitive dissonance, and premature cognitive closure. We see what we want to see, and often can't see the wood through the trees. We can also only debate a matter so long; we have to take mental shortcuts so that we can move on. We tend to see the world through the prism of our own beliefs, values, biases and prejudices. When we look for evidence of Weapons of Mass Destruction in Iraq, we find that evidence of absence is not absence of evidence. It is called confirmation bias.

CADET 1: In addition our view of the outside world is subjective. The brain gets us to see something in a particular way because for whatever reason it was useful to do so in the past: it gave us a competitive advantage in the struggle for survival. We are the product of our Stone Age brains—so evolutionary psychologists tell us.

CADET 3: And the brain is constantly referring back to the most recent events in our lives. If you look at a bright stimulus and then look away and close your eyes, what do you see—its complementary colour. Observing a bright green image leaves a red image imprinted on your vision. So what you see beforehand might well change the colour you see, just as in going back to history to find analogies for current situations invariably we appeal to the recent past even if it is not especially illuminating.

CADET 2: In other words, General, we can never penetrate the reality of war, only approximations of reality.

INSTRUCTOR: That is why we tell the cadets that the aim of any theory is not to draw a map of the world, but to point us in the right direction. Of course, that's not what many people think it is. They often mistake the map for the territory; they confuse the model of reality with reality itself. The map is not the thing mapped. Maps are made from representations of the terrain. Every theory in that sense is only a representation of a map, but it is invaluable if it is that it is a good representation, if it has structure analogous to the territory.

This is why your use of metaphors is so instructive. Here is one of the most famous sayings from your book that we at the Academy very much take to heart: 'I shall not begin by formulating a crude, journalistic definition of war but go straight to the heart of the matter, to the duel. War is nothing but a duel on a larger scale.' (*On War*, 1, 2). Later, you compare it to a wrestling match. One of the features of your work, General, for which you are famous, is your use of metaphors. Several of your concepts such as 'friction', 'polarity' and 'centre of gravity' were drawn from what we call physics and what in your day was known as the 'mechanical sciences'. If we read your original text we find that the centre of gravity expressed primarily as *Schwerpunkt* ('the main point') appears more than fifty times (Echevarria, 2003, 110).

Recently I gave one of the cadets an assignment to write a paper on the importance of metaphor in the formulation of theory. Perhaps you would allow him to speak to it now?

CLAUSEWITZ: Of course.

CADET 2: In my paper, General, I explained that scientists tell us that language itself is a metaphorical expression of human experience. Events 'happen' so we understand causation. Action can be initiated only with a 'goal' in mind. We tend to think of a goal as a destination because we walk towards something we want, and we tend to think of time as a moving object because things that approach us get closer. In both cases, they are rooted in physical existence (Pinker, 2007, 245).

INSTRUCTOR: The metaphors that we invoke today might well differ from yours, General, but your two most important: war as a duel and a clash of wills seem to me to be still operative. One side can be said to have prevailed over another because its will to win is greater, but that of course can be attributed to many factors: moral (self-belief); technical (superior technology); cultural (social resilience in the case of a long drawn-out conflict); heroic (the call to arms). The great mistake is to get the metaphor to do all the thinking for us so that we fall back upon the idea that Napoleon alone 'willed' victory or that the French Revolutionary armies were sustained entirely by what Georges Sorel called 'intelligent bayonets'. The citizen-army may have been a necessary condition of success, but it was not a sufficient one. Other factors came into play, such as the reorganisation of the army into a Corps system (which allowed every corps to operate independently for up to 48 hours). And the French armies disposed of superior technology—in addition to muskets some soldiers were issued with rifle-carbines which were lighter and smaller, and ideal weapons for snipers and sharpshooters. But then the devil is always in the detail.

CADET 2: In my essay I wrote that there are always two difficulties in using metaphors—first there is the boundary problem, where the literal ends and the figurative begins. Secondly there is the dilemma: where the literal interpretation of a term comes to strain belief, and the alternative is that it is metaphorical, what is the metaphor for? (Lloyd, 2012, 86); When the world changes, so should we. We should 'cash in' our metaphors for others. Metaphors, in William James' sense, have 'cash-value', and we must always be careful not to trade in a debased currency. But their shelf life is often longer than we might suppose. To call war a duel allows us to invoke different styles of duelling— a fight to the death, a ritualistic exercise, even a balletic *pas de deux*. To call war a clash of wills is to accept that there are different styles of willing and different things to will—Nietzsche tells us that modern man can even will nothingness.

INSTRUCTOR: I think the main point, General, is that as metaphors go, yours have never been bettered; for the most part they still hold true. But we must always recognise that even the most compelling metaphors are not like historical analogies or parallels. They are not identities, but similarities, and if we define war as a duel or wrestling match, that is to suggest implicitly that there are also differences between them, and it is by identifying the differences that we have a chance of understanding what war actually is.

We can't dispense with metaphors for another reason: they are central to the belief that it is possible to define the essence of a phenomenon. What is the essence of war, you ask? 'War is ... an act of force to compel an enemy to do our will.' (*On War*, 1, 2). It would seem we are hard-wired to see the essence of everything. At a very early age children make categorical distinctions between cats and dogs that go beyond outward appearance. If they see a puppy or kitten, they know it will grow up to be a dog or a cat, even if a puppy is raised in a litter of kittens. The psychologist Paul Bloom believes that we invest objects (both non-animate or inanimate) with an essential quality with which we can bond. Philosophers, too, talk of an 'ens' or 'quiddity', an invisible property which (say) all teddy bears have. These may not be real properties, like the properties of copper (a chemical element with a symbol Cu and the atomic number 29, a soft, malleable and ductile material with very high thermal and electrical conductivity). Yet philosophical and popular definitions are real enough. They are psychological constructs in which we invest enormous emotional capital (Hood, 2013, 139). And in turn they make possible the invention of theory without which there can be no reflective human life.

OK let's move to the second question: why do theory?

Slide 2

WHY DO THEORY?

- Why did you choose theory?
- What are the main theoretical propositions of your work: what's the message?
- Can theory help you win?

CLAUSEWITZ: I should come clean at this point and admit that I first set out to come up with a few, precise, compact set of propositions. I originally set out to write a standard manual on war. But I have long ago concluded that it's in my nature to systematise, to work things through. Thus I ended up proposing a series of general rules that would aid judgement and help an able commander to win a war (all things being equal which in war is rarely the case!).

My greatest mistake was to set out to write a theory of war predicated almost entirely on my own experience of the battlefield. It was only quite late in the day—in 1827, in fact—that I set out to correct this initial short-sightedness. I am afraid I was guilty of the besetting sin of military theorists: to think that one's own experience is all that really counts. In reality, every war is very different.

INSTRUCTOR: We call it 'presentism'—the abiding sin of thinking that the present is the most important moment in history, the departure point for everything in the future. But can you give the cadets an example of the dangers of taking a theory too literally?

CLAUSEWITZ: Well, as you all know I placed particular emphasis on bringing the enemy to battle. Later, I saw that Napoleon's pursuit of the decisive battle had led inevitably to his eventual undoing in Russia. How could a real battlefield success, which of course eluded him, have changed anything if the Russians

continued to trade space for time? The Russian campaign illustrates the problem of not thinking through
war enough. Unfortunately, Napoleon had very little
interest in theory. In the sixty battles he fought, he
once confessed, he learned nothing new (McLynn,
1997, 145). That was his problem. The longer he was
in the field the more his enemies learned from his
mistakes; eventually they discovered a certain 'formula' to his war making. They even discovered his
principal weakness—what one of your contemporary
historians calls 'the imp of the perverse', which mani-
fested itself in a deliberate decision to leave certain
things to chance, almost as though he was pushing his
luck. His genius, of course, was his ability to impro-
vise when things went wrong, but improvisation
doesn't help that much when they go very wrong, as
they did in the 1812 campaign.

INSTRUCTOR: OK, can you identify what you consider to be your
most important theoretical propositions.

CLAUSEWITZ: Let me identify three. The first is the difference
between the nature of war and its character. We have
a common nature, but we all live different historical
lives and forge different historical experiences.

INSTRUCTOR: So what is the nature of war?

Perhaps, I can kick off by drawing the cadets' attention to a concept made famous by one of the twentieth
century's greatest philosophers, Ludwig Wittgenstein:
his concept of family resemblances. The example he
offers is that of games. What do games share in common? They are, after all, so very different. There are
games in which the ball is whacked across a field, or
pitched by a baseball player, or thumped into a goal
by foot, or in the case of hockey by a stick. Some of
these games involve one player (golf), most involve a
team. In some you compete against yourself (in lawn
tennis unforced errors are as important as forced

errors); in others you face a hostile and hopefully spirited opponent. And that's just one set of games—ball games. Games cover everything from poker to Formula 1 racing and the triathlon at the Olympics. When we call them games, added Wittgenstein, we are invoking 'a complicated network of similarities overlapping and criss-crossing' (*Philosophical Investigations*, para. 66).

He then went on to compare this tangled web of affinities to family resemblances. Take a Navajo family structure—with its grandparents, grandchildren, cousins (many or not, several times removed), not to forget the resident PhD anthropologist doing field-work (Laughter). Yes, I'm joking. With the exception of the anthropologist every member is related, but will differ in height, facial features and even tempera-ment. But an astute outside observer may see family lineages in a way that so far a computer programmed with face recognition algorithms still can't.

The concept of family resemblance is not without its critics, of course. And they pack some powerful punches. If everything has the same resemblance to something else, what's the difference between them? Neither a fly nor a typewriter has an imagination, for example. But the point is that you don't have to give up the idea of essence in taking up Wittgenstein's idea (Cavell, 1979, 186). In fact, argues Stanley Cavell, Wittgenstein is not out to discredit the notion of essence but to rescue it. Essence is contained in gram-mar, Wittgenstein argues, meaning that it is the rules that govern the way we apply words which tell us what a thing is. Cavell also holds that Wittgenstein is not advancing the family resemblance idea as an alter-native to those who believe in universal natures (since for one thing a universalist might ask for the essential meaning of this very idea). Nor is he proposing that this model is enough to explain naming, meaning and so on. Wittgenstein wants to wean us off universals and persuade us that they are not especially useful or necessary.

CLAUSEWITZ: Interesting. All grammar has a function, of course. If, as I claim, war is—or should be—a 'political' phenomenon then we must distinguish it from other acts of violence that are non-political, such as piracy. Now, it's a little complicated. You see piracy can be an instrument of war, as it was in the seventeen and eighteenth centuries. States often empowered their citizens to act as privateers and issued government licences for the capture of enemy shipping. Some pirates even had their own charters (or social contracts); they called themselves commonwealths; every pirate had a vote on a ship (Tilly, 2005, 81–4); they often looked like states. But of course piracy as an activity is quite distinct from the political realm. Its only purpose is individual profit.

INSTRUCTOR: Carl Schmitt brings this out clearly in his essay *The Theory of the Partisan* (1962). The pirate, he writes, is possessed of what in jurisprudence is known as *animus furandi* (felonious intent). The partisan—the insurgent, the national liberation fighter—the non-state actor (or terrorist) fights on a political front. In German *partisan* means 'a party adherent' and Schmitt reminds us that the word 'partisan', unlike 'pirate' has a multiplicity of meanings. In English, the word 'partisan' means 'to take sides.' It's this changing set of meanings which makes it such a politically charged word. (Schmitt 1962/2004)

CLAUSEWITZ: So, wars employ violence in pursuit of different purposes. Some involve conquest; some annihilation (the destruction of Carthage in 146 BC). Some states set out to punish transgressors against the international order of the day; some wish merely to restore the balance of power, while others wish to subvert it. No war, to my knowledge, has ever been meaningless.

INSTRUCTOR: And here we come to your principal claim: war is an instrument of politics by an admixture of other means (*On War*, 8, 6b). It's not an original insight I hope you won't mind me saying, General; it was shared by some of your contemporaries at the War Academy in Berlin. The true originality of your claim lies elsewhere. But to stick to the word you employed— *Politik*. What does that word actually mean? Can we try to unpack it?

CLAUSEWITZ: When you cadets first entered the military profession, I imagine you thought of war as a three stage affair: attack, fight or flight, win or lose. Soldiers tend to think of war in terms of combat, but combat is 'only the price of admission' to a war (Strauss, 2012, 3). When you go to war you have to look beyond the battlefield—to decide not only how to fight, but who to fight, and why you should in the first place. You have to define what you understand by victory and thus know when to end the war and so design a postwar settlement that will make victory long-lasting. For even when you win a victory, you have to know how to use it, that is, to translate it into political capital, and that's often the most challenging task of all.

Politics doesn't end when the shooting starts; it determines who we are shooting at, and how deadly is our aim. It determines the end objective and what kind of peace we hope to fashion after the shooting stops. And here is the key passage again from Book 8 of *On War*: 'Do political relations between peoples and their governments stop when diplomatic notes are no longer exchanged? Is war not just another expression of their thoughts, another expression of speech and writing? Its grammar indeed may be its own, but not its logic.' (*On War*, 8, 6b). As long as the political dimension persists, as it usually does in most conflict between states, war won't follow its own logic, that is, its tendency towards the absolute, its tendency to follow its own 'laws', which is why you should always try to ensure that war takes its cue from politics and policy and that you concern yourself with immediate probabilities.

INSTRUCTOR: So, that little word *Politik* packs quite a punch! OK, you have mentioned two key concerns of yours: escalation and politics. The two are often connected, are they not?

CLAUSEWITZ: Indeed. Let me take escalation. The tendency for war to escalate may depend at least in part on the political milieu. The French Revolutionary Wars, which so impressed me at the time, were the product of a revolutionary mind-set. Later, Napoleon was able to harness a revolutionary spirit to test the limits of his own destiny. My compatriot Heine saw him once riding into the city of Dusseldorf. He later came to see Napoleon as a numinous historical figure whose very example had changed history forever: he had shown that through war it was possible to pursue a revolutionary vision. Another of my contemporaries, the poet Hölderlin, even spoke of 'the spiritual violence of the times.'

CADET 1: General, the Russian novelist Dostoevsky makes the same point in *Crime and Punishment*. The anti-hero Raskolnikov identifies especially with what he calls Napoleon's 'criminality' or, we might say, his refusal to be constrained by conventional social norms. He applauds the fact that he 'carries out a massacre in Paris, forgets an army in Egypt, wastes half a million men in the Moscow campaign. ...' (Dostoyevsky, 1951, 291). In 1813 Napoleon shocked the Austrian Chancellor Metternich by saying 'Do you think I give a shit about the loss of a million men?'

INSTRUCTOR: Carl Schmitt was insistent that all military theory must start with the understanding of enmity—is the enemy an existential threat or merely an instrumental one; can we live with the enemy after the war is won, or must we exterminate him, or domesticate him, or win him over to our cause. Unless we understand what—not merely who—the enemy is, all attempts to ring-fence war morally are merely disingenuous (Schmitt, 1962/2004, 64). Historians largely attribute the barbarity of warfare to the 'barbarian tendencies' in twentieth century political life. Remember that the gas chambers at Auschwitz were originally built to kill Polish resistance fighters, then Soviet POWs.

INSTRUCTOR: So, here's the thing—does the tendency towards the absolute not also inhere in war itself?

CLAUSEWITZ: Both readings are permissible because this at different times is actually what I wrote.

Real war can, and must, involve an absolute logic: the destruction of the enemy force, so to prevent escalation and to end the war quickly. But the destruction of an enemy force or the complete disarmament of an enemy country—for example the unconditional surrender of Germany and Japan in 1945—falls far short of a war aim such as the elimination of a state or the total destruction of its social and economic life.

INSTRUCTOR: Of course, this leaves you with a dilemma, doesn't it? How can limited objectives break the escalatory tendency towards absolute war? And how limited are aims if the realistic destruction of an enemy force requires operations to be prolonged in order to effect it? The more you aim for the total destruction of its army, surely the more likely the enemy will fight on?

By the way there is one war that comes very near to your theory of absolute war. It was the war between

Paraguay and its neighbours in 1865. Paraguay lost four fifths of its territory and 70 per cent of its population. The ratio of men to women at the war's end was 1:20. Young children were used to retrieve cannon balls that had failed to explode and often lost their lives as they were returning to the lines. Libraries were ransacked so that the paper in the books could be used as fuses.

CLAUSEWITZ: That illustrates the importance of another concept of mine:

War is fought to empower one of the parties: to win markets; to expand territory; to spread ideas. War can also involve the power to reverse history (for example to avenge a defeat). These are all reasons why states may find themselves at war but they don't help explain the final decision to go to war (Blanning, 1986, 27).

So, ladies and gentlemen, you may well ask why two states contest the issue if one clearly has superior resources, as was clearly the case in the example your instructor has just provided. The answer is that often they evaluate power very differently.

INSTRUCTOR: If I may give the cadets an example. Hitler went to war thinking that the Aryan race had a greater capacity for sacrifice than any other. Unfortunately for him, every war involves a large element of the mundane. Germany had lost the war strategically by December 1941, and although a tactical and operational collapse on all three Fronts in Russia was narrowly averted in January–March 1942, it was never able to really recapture the strategic initiative. The reason was quite simple: it might indeed have disposed of greater will power but not of the number of men it needed to take on the Russians. After December 1941 the *Ostwehr* could only be reinforced by an additional five infantry divisions. The Red Army was

43

still over 4 million strong. The German Army can be said to have lost the Second World War on the intellectual plane long before it was defeated on the material one (Magenheimer, 1998, 277).

CLAUSEWITZ: In other words, wars are often the result of misjudgement—misjudging one's own power or underestimating that of the enemy. And one of the greatest miscalculations of all comes from thinking that wars won't last long. It's doubtful whether any war since 1700 has come about with both sides believing that it would be particularly protracted (Blainey, 1973, 246). I am pretty sure you would not have got yourselves into Afghanistan had you known it would be the longest war in your history.

CADET 2: So, General, power is the essence of war?

CLAUSEWITZ: No. War is about power, as is practically everything else in life. But its essence is violence, and all violence requires a grammar. What is important is what violence says or communicates. If you make it to Book 8 of my work you will find that I claim that 'war has its own grammar, but not its own logic.' (*On War*, 8, 6b). In this case grammar is not violence but its language and that language is culturally defined—it is to be found in military doctrines that you learn in Academies like this, or that much earlier in history were codified by custom, like those that Thucydides called 'the common customs of the Greeks.' And like most rules they usually benefit a particular social order of the day. The beneficiaries in the case of the early classical period in Greece were the heavily armoured infantry, the Hoplites who did the bulk of the fighting. The rules meant that battles were lethal, but the casualties were limited, which was necessary to ensure that the Hoplite class in the Greek city-states remained the gravitational centre of Greek life.

INSTRUCTOR: Many thanks for this clarification, General. But as time is pressing, can we move onto another concept—that of the trinity. Can we—so to say—put it in dry dock to see what is beneath the surface of the concept? In the first trinity you tell us that war involves passion, reason and the play of probabilities (or chance). Now I think there's no presumption that any one of these is more important than the other (although we tend to privilege reason these days). But where, General, does this idea derive from?

CLAUSEWITZ: I know some people think it's a religious conception: after all, I am the grandson of a Lutheran pastor. Some people think that because I am also a Christian that I got the idea from the Christian Trinity, which defines God as three persons, expressions, or hypostases (underlying states): the Father, Son and Holy Ghost. Three persons who are distinct, yet of one substance, essence or nature. All three are one, and each is all three.

INSTRUCTOR: And whereas the doctrine of the Trinity in Christianity is intended to bring humanity face to face with the mystery of God, you propose to bring us face to face with the mystery of war (you do use the word 'mystery' from time to time, you know).

CADET 3: Actually, we've noticed in the class that you have a propensity to see issues in terms of threes: three reasons for having a strong vanguard in the centre; three conditions under which armies should be quartered; three spatially distinct bases of operation (Strachan and Herberg-Rohte, 2007, 85–6).

INSTRUCTOR: Your whole approach can be said to involve the principle of trichotomy (the three-way classification or division that is such a marked feature of European philosophy).

CLAUSEWITZ: Such as?

INSTRUCTOR: Well, you find it in Plato's *Republic*—the first great thought-experiment in philosophy. In his ideal state reason is represented by the state; spiritedness by the army (the guardians); and desire by the merchants. You also find the principle at work in Aristotle's three kinds of causes: preconditions, precipitants and triggers; in Augustine's three laws, the divine, natural and human; and of course in Kant's whole philosophy, but especially his division of higher cognition into understanding, judgement and reason. Surely what you were trying to do is what all scientists try to do: to summarise the results of a vast number of experiments and observations in terms of a few powerful laws. Or, in today's language, to produce the shortest possible program that outputs the world.

Anyway, this is largely peripheral to our discussion. This version of the trinity, by the way, has only really been studied in depth since the 1970s.

CLAUSEWITZ: Might I be permitted a few words to explain what I meant by the trinity? No-one starts a war without a reason, a purpose, or a goal. War is also sustained by the passions, or what you called 'moral forces' such as hatred and courage. You have to persuade people to kill but it is even more challenging to persuade them to put their lives on the line. These are the two human factors that come up against chance or contingency, the unpredictable in life. The point is that if reason and passion and chance are in balance you stand a better chance of maintaining political control.

INSTRUCTOR: Too much reason—our own over-reliance in Vietnam on 'capture-kill' ratios and body counts and computer models lost us that war; and too much hatred of subhuman Slavs lost Germany the Second World War.

CLAUSEWITZ: And you are now in danger of introducing ultimate rationality into war: killer robots.

INSTRUCTOR: Well, a near contemporary of yours, Soren Kierke-gaard, predicted that just as metaphysics had replaced theology so physics would eventually replace moral reflection.

CLAUSEWITZ: Yes, that was my fear too when it came to war. In my book I warned against the idea of conducting war by algebra; I was horrified at the prospect that instru-mental rationality might dominate military thinking. If reason came to outweigh everything else truth would no longer be what we feel in our pulses. Out would go glory, the joy of fighting, and the thrill of combat. To a civilian this might sound fine; in reality if the scientists took over you might end up with hardened hearts and deadened minds.

INSTRUCTOR: Can we move to the other trinity: the idea that war involves three elements; the government, the army and the people. In your day you could assume with a fair degree of confidence that when a state went to war against another all three elements would feed off each other in a kind of cybernetic loop. A state was only as strong as the army to defend it and an army was only as strong as the people on whom it can draw.

CLAUSEWITZ: Take the French revolutionary wars. Once a people could be engaged politically they could be con-scripted. The army was transformed as well—it could now outnumber its enemies. Napoleon nearly always disposed of superior numbers, though in the end he ran out of men. And the state, of course, was able to be far more ambitious in setting political aims.

CADET 1: It is often claimed today that the trinity breaks down in our ever more complex world.

CLAUSEWITZ: I've given this idea some thought during my stay here. Look, you make far too much of this. What makes war today more complex than in the past is the fact that political actors tend to multiply.

INSTRUCTOR: I think that is absolutely right. Social situations become more complex once additional actors appear, such as NATO in Afghanistan, or additional factors such as the global opium market or the global small arms market that emerged after the collapse of Communism in 1989. This makes it necessary for the locals to master several different roles at once. And here's another thing. In some cases these groups take shape in reality, but only after they have been defined in theory. They come together because they are bribed to be on side; they assume the roles they do because it makes them money. The people remain— you even try these days to win their hearts and minds and craft the right 'narrative'; but the concept itself has become more multifaceted.

But what of the army?

CLAUSEWITZ: Several 'armies' can be fighting each other at the same time, but whether they are irregulars or conventional soldiers, heavily armed NATO forces or Taliban, they are armies of a kind.

INSTRUCTOR: Yes, at first glance in Syria it all looks very confusing. Russian money, Iranian advisers, and Hezbollah fighters on the ground hold the Syrian Army together. The Iraqi Army is fighting ISIS but so too is the Kurdish Peshmerga of Northern Iraq, with volunteers from abroad.

CLAUSEWITZ: And there is usually a state authority of some kind, you know, however beleaguered it may find itself.

INSTRUCTOR: Well, that's a lot for the students to take in. But time is pressing and we need to move on to the last two questions. How to do theory?

Slide 3

HOW TO DO THEORY

- What is its 'value-added'?
- What is the importance of psychology?
- What is the value of the imagination?

INSTRUCTOR: I would like to turn to what is value-added in your work—the importance of emotions. Jesse Glenn Gray once wrote that there is no other human experience like war that is associated with such a wide range of emotions. 'It compresses the greatest opposites into the smallest space in the shortest time.' (Gray, 1998, 12). Taking a very different tack, Edward Wilson complains that we concentrate too much on our emotional life. Science tells us much about the nature of existence, but the humanities, he adds, 'only deal with the relatively small range of human emotions.' (Wilson, 2014). It's not a view, I imagine, to which you would be sympathetic.

CLAUSEWITZ: Absolutely not. Emotions are highly complex. Let me take courage. In my book I identified three different kinds (*On War*, 3, 6). One, indifference to danger; two, boldness; three, resolution. Indifference to danger encourages recklessness, rather than reasoned risk-taking. Boldness is the willingness to take informed risks. Resolution, or what I called *courage d'esprit*, is the ability to make a decision quickly and stick with it in the face of all setbacks. This, too, is an emotional state of mind. So we have before us three different kinds of courage—a willingness to risk all; an indifference to danger; and finally the resolution to soldier on. Actually, I was not particularly interested in the first two; I took them for granted because they can be drilled in through routine and because war tends to attract that kind of person. What interested me most was the third: resolution, the courage demanded of every commander.

Interestingly, there was increasing stress in my day on the mental qualities, on strong nerves (Harari, 2008, 199). You know, I wrote of four types of commanders, all in psychological terms—the phlegmatic (who are rarely roused to anger); the extremely active, who nonetheless tend to be calm in the face of danger; those whose passions are easily inflamed but soon burn out; and those who are not easily moved, but whose emotions are strongly grounded. These four personality types, I insisted, were probably accounted for by the nervous system (but obviously the science of the day did not enable me to understand it as you do now).

INSTRUCTOR: You were certainly in step with the times, if not ahead of them, though your contemporaries did not speak of emotions so much as 'feelings', 'affections', 'appetites', 'passions' and sometimes 'moral sentiments'.

CLAUSEWITZ: Yes, you are right, though I have never really thought of that before. I did indeed talk about the ability to master the passions in the heat of battle. Perhaps, where I differed from most of my contemporaries was in seeing self-control as an emotion or a feeling, or what I called 'the energy of the mind' and at other times the 'energy of the soul.' The ability to subordinate anger to the needs of others is informed by an emotional need—to be honoured by others; to be esteemed for the self-control that others lack (Lehrer, 2009).

INSTRUCTOR: Some psychologists would say that this is more a life-strategy than an emotion.

CLAUSEWITZ: Aren't all life-strategies emotional?

INSTRUCTOR: To be sure. Can I draw your attention to a new field of cognitive science known as 'embodied cognition.' Back in the seventeenth century an anatomist called Thomas Willis was the first person to propose that the experience of 'trembling with fear' or 'bursting with joy' might be the effect not of liquids in the body but of latticework in the brain (Smith, 2015). We now know how all our tissues and organs play a role in our feelings. Thanks to neuroscience we now know how richly endowed the human body is in nerves and other cells that communicate through chemical and electrical signalling. The brain, we are told, is more like a chatroom where information is shared than a command and control centre.

Let me try to sum up what we know so far. Our understanding of emotions is governed by two approaches—cultural anthropology and socio-biology—which were not taught in your day, General. The first school views emotions as cultural constructions: we are only allowed to show emotions which are culturally permissible. Sometimes we're allowed to cry in public, sometimes we're expected to hold back our tears. These are what anthropologists call 'social masks', or 'rules of conduct' which ensure social conformity.

The historian William Reddy also writes of 'emotional regimes'. We all live in them, whether we admit to it or not. Take flight attendants who have to smile because the passengers expect it. But baseball coaches are famous for their angry outbursts. And in any social setting if you transgress the rules you get fired or demoted or excluded, or at the very least become the subject of gossip. Reddy interprets the French Revolution as an effort to overthrow an existing regime of emotional restraint in favour of a new and unstable 'sentimental logic'. And he speculates that the French Revolutionary armies on their march through Europe can be said to have been animated not so much by the revolutionary ideas: liberty, fraternity and equality as by emotional excess (Plamper, 2010).

The second school views emotions as the default mode for animals trying to survive in a hostile environment. This understanding owes much to Darwin. You should read his much-neglected book *The Expression of the Emotions in Man and Animals* (1872). But its most famous adherent today is probably Joseph LeDoux (*The Two Roads of Fear*). LeDoux tells us that the emotions are biological functions channelled through the amygdalae, which trigger emotional responses. Semantic markers are associations between reinforcing stimuli that induce an associated physiological effective state that can influence cognitive processes (that is, decision making).

I apologise, General. I know it is very complicated. I had to look all this up myself. All I am saying is that you really did revolutionise our thinking about war in emphasising the importance of moral and psychological factors. Even the importance you attached to the fervour of the French revolutionary armies is something that has been borne out by modern science.

CADET 2:   I wonder if you can explain what you meant by genius, Sir?

CLAUSEWITZ: A genius is a man who by definition is in some way or another larger than the situation he inherits.

INSTRUCTOR: Let me give you one example. A Russian officer explained the failure of General Bennigsten to win the Battle of Eylau (1807) as a failure of inspirational insight. Bennigsten, he claimed, had a mind that was quite equal to the task of grappling with similar minds, but he couldn't deal with genius, 'that inexplicable impulse which is as instantaneous as an electric spark' (Harari, 2008, 157). Note the imagery— Napoleon thought of himself as an 'electric discharge', a man who could metaphorically electrify the men under his command.

CLAUSEWITZ: Yes indeed. I actually called intuition a flash of lightning which arises unconsciously and not within logical chains of thought (*On War*, 1, 3). I said that genius is felt, it's not deduced. The insights achieved are very different from those achieved through deductive reasoning.

CADET 4: So might I ask both of you just how much of a genius was Napoleon?

INSTRUCTOR: Well, that depends on what you understand by the term. One definition is being able to see opportunities which others don't. Let me give you an example—the victory that established his career and took him from an artillery captain to Brigadier General overnight. I'm talking about the capture of Toulon in 1793. The British had occupied the port and captured half the French Navy. They couldn't be easily dislodged and the longer they stayed, the more the French Revolutionary cause was in danger. But Napoleon saw the British had a critical vulnerability: re-supplying their own fleet. And only he noticed two small, highly-guarded forts on a hill overlooking the harbour. Taking them wouldn't help him dislodge the British by force, but it would help him control the movement of shipping into and out of the harbour. And although heavy cannon—then still the mainstay of artillery power—could not give the forts the firepower they needed to threaten the ships, light artillery could. Eventually the British were forced to evacuate the harbour.

Now, the point of the story is this. What Napoleon saw is what he already knew: that the British had been forced to lift the Siege of Boston in 1776 and surrender Yorktown in 1781 in the American Revolutionary War when they, too, had their supply routes challenged. But the point is that only he saw it and therefore only he could access and apply this knowledge (Klein, 2014, 89–90).

CLAUSEWITZ: We might also think of genius, perhaps, not so much as an analytical form of decision-making as a different way of using experience to quickly frame situations, size them up and know what to do next. It is experience that allows some men to see behavioural patterns that others can't.

And on that basis you can make intuitive decisions. You can gamble on instinct. I called it 'tact of judgement.' It involves the ability to weigh up options, and find the one that is probably likely to succeed. In a short passage I wrote about Political Calculation (1808), I talked about probability at greater length. I said that it's the ability of a general to negotiate the 'labyrinth of alternatives' and select the right course. Note, not 'right' in the objective sense for his final judgement call may well be wrong. But his mistake, if he is wrong, will remain improbable nonetheless (Engberg-Pedersen, 2015, 79).

Let us also take Napoleon's intuitive grasp of the importance of what you Americans call 'Shock and Awe'. Napoleon invented the concept, you know. What his enemies found they lacked was not brave soldiers or even competent commanders; they lacked a concept that could bring together in harmony two key elements in battle: fear and force. Force can be simply defined in terms of mass and velocity, or visible, demonstrable power. Napoleon attacked in columns which were frightening because they were visible. Speed was also vital. Napoleon was a master of operational speed (getting to the battlefield quickly), as well as tactical speed (or manoeuvring on it) (Bateman 1999, 26). In the case of Jena, speed came after the battle in the ruthlessness of the chase following the collapse of primary group cohesion. We Prussians put up almost no resistance.

Our demoralisation was total. This made the defeat particularly shameful, of course.

The other component of Napoleon's shock tactics was fear: the fear inspired by mass formations in close order, marching in-step. The cry of 'Vive L'Empereur' demonstrably unsettled the enemy.

CADET 4:   So if Napoleon was such a genius, why did he fail?

CLAUSEWITZ: A good question, young man. And let me volunteer an answer, or an attempt at one. It was because of his genius, not in spite of it. A paradox? Of course, but then life is deeply paradoxical, so what's new? When we observe the world around us what do we see? It is deeply unfair. The profligate wins the lottery; the wrong man goes to jail, which is why we talk about fate and destiny and the stars (we love astrology for that reason). Napoleon was a supreme gambler who, like all addicts, didn't know when to quit. And as you keep winning—often against the odds—so you come to believe you are the instrument of destiny.

And that was his eventual undoing. In my book I wrote that his victory at the Battle of Lodi in 1796 was the decisive moment in his career—the moment in which a man knows once and for all who he is. It was an unnecessary battle, as it happens, because the Austrian army was already in retreat. It could not have contested the crossing of the bridge the following day. It was a mistake on Napoleon's part because he thought he was attacking the main force of the enemy when he was only attacking its rear-guard. It was actually a failure because he failed to bring about the decisive battle that he wanted to determine the fate of Italy once and for all. But it changed Napoleon profoundly. Just think about it: to force a bridge only 300 paces long against an army of 7,000 men with fourteen guns convinced Napoleon that he was a 'winner' (Blanning, 1996, 146–7). As I wrote in my book: 'he was drunk with victory'; 'He was in an elevated state of hope, courage and confidence' which never left him. Lodi transformed Napoleon—it transformed his understanding of what he could do; it made him more ambitious (Klein, 2014, 22–23).

But of course Napoleon the gambler wouldn't quit even when he was ahead. And you all know what happened.

INSTRUCTOR: OK. Let's move on.

Slide 4

WHAT DOES THEORY ACHIEVE?

• Is war becoming too complex to theorise?

INSTRUCTOR: Has war become too complex to theorise?

CLAUSEWITZ: A theory, remember, should offer a critical engagement with the world of common sense. It should do away with the received wisdoms of the day. It should clear the mind. If it does all these then it will have achieved a lot. Its purpose, remember, is not to make you happy. Its purpose is to remind you how little you still know. All we can hold onto are those rules and regularities, those principles, or what I sometimes mistakenly called 'laws', which allow us to see the continuities in war, while helping us to adjust to the discontinuities we continually encounter in life. I suspect that wars of the future are going to demand the same skills, however complex the general picture.

CADET 4: Does your own theory tell us anything about the future?

CLAUSEWITZ: It is true that that my critics like to fault me for not predicting the revolution in rifle power after 1840 or trench warfare to come. But how could I? Was it a failure of imagination to anticipate industrialised war-

CLAUSEWITZ AT WEST POINT

fare, or the ideologies of total war in the twentieth century? Not at all. If I'd been able to imagine them, I would have brought them into existence.

But please don't think of the future as many of you tend to do by back-projecting to the past. For example what if Robert E. Lee had drones at his disposal at the Battle of Gettysburg? Would he have launched Pickett's charge up Cemetery Ridge if he'd known that this was not an especially weak point in the Union's army line? What if the British had satellite reconnaissance at the Somme (1916)? Would they have launched a mass 'suicidal' frontal assault? What if you'd had streaming video of Japanese forces fortifying bunkers in Okinawa—would you have tried to take the Shuri Line in a frontal assault? (Hanson, 2010, 115–116). All of these assume that the Germans couldn't have destroyed the satellites, or the Japanese jammed the video feeds, or for that matter that the Union couldn't have brought down the drones. It is because I took history seriously that I couldn't make wild guesses about the future.

But these parlour games at least show how the character of war constantly changes over time. For you don't find mass infantry attacks in an age of satellites, you have mass armoured attacks which the Soviets planned to launch had the Cold War gone hot. You don't see many mass infantry assaults in an age of video-streaming because you don't have much mass. The process isn't entirely linear, of course, and it's not necessarily 'progressive', but there does seem to be a direction in war, at least since the beginning of the gunpowder age. So look for the trends of your own age. Trend analysis is the only method we have of anticipating future trends within—I would like to think—the conceptual framework that I offer in my book.

CADET 3:   Sorry, Sir, might I ask the professor one last question?

INSTRUCTOR: Go on.

CLAUSEWITZ: Let me remind you, I'm not a professor.

CADET 4: Sorry, General, what do you think of zombies? (Laughter)

CLAUSEWITZ: I have been told that at the Academy you spend a lot of time reading zombie novels and playing computer games in which they figure. And I would urge you to continue doing so. The problem young people joining the military now face is that the military profession is becoming so disenchanting. The problem with so much military theory today is that it's big on data, but thin on story-telling. And that's why I suspect you like game-playing because it's all about narratives; it's all about setting the scene, and locating people in a time and history that means something to you. A theory must never lose sight of the human dimension of life. We Germans have two words: *Erfahrung*, what happens to me, and *Erlebnis*, what I live through. One involves information that is unprocessed, the other information that is processed. One is external to an actor; the other is internal to his thoughts, emotions and impressions of the world. We should never lose sight of 'lived experience'; it's the most important experience of all.

INSTRUCTOR: Actually, when General Dempsey addressed us in 2013 he told the cadets that after reading Max Brook's novel *World War Z* he'd gone to the Chiefs of Staff and asked them what to do if the zombies actually appeared. (Dempsey 2013)

CADET 4: Yeah, and you know the Pentagon now has a battle plan for a zombie attack? It's an unclassified document CONOP8888 that was originally drawn up by Strategic Command? (Pentagon, Zombies)

INSTRUCTOR: All these plans, of course, are meant only to bring home to people the challenge of global pandemics, and to help hospitals and other agencies draw up contingency plans to meet them.

CLAUSEWITZ: Don't be so defensive! We had zombies too. Think of Mary Shelley's *Frankenstein*, which came out during my lifetime. But let us be serious for a moment.

In real life war tends to bring out the best both in our enemies and ourselves. We are both forced to think more imaginatively, to act more daringly and to defy the odds. In a word, we are forced to learn, whether we wish to or not. I too have read *World War Z*. It was recommended to me when I first arrived at the academy. Remember how you get to win—by playing your ace card: culture. Like us, zombies have needs (they are hungry all the time). But unlike us they have no desires, ambitions or aspirations. Because they have no culture they cannot diversify their tactics, or win by outguessing us. Human beings, by contrast, have ways of warfare, cultural styles of waging it that are ethnocentric. Different societies tend to look at the world from their own vantage points and see their enemies within their own frames of reference. Zombies, on the other hand, fill their ranks from every culture and none. They are what we Germans call *Kulturlos*.

So, what does Mr Brooks tell us in his novel? Humanity gets to win by stepping back in time. Soldiers once again march in column. The primary weapon is once again the standard rifle. Soldiers stand or kneel in straight lines in two ranks like the reinforced squares found on the battlefields of my day. In the United States you have to re-learn the old skills. You go back to the Frontier wars against the Indians. The Europeans, by contrast, take to fortresses and castles where they are able to last out not only for weeks, but for months.

You asked me a moment ago whether there had ever been an absolute war. World War Z would perhaps be it. For it demands no half measures. I suspect the real reason that you like reading about zombies is that the war against them is morally unambiguous—it is apolitical. There are no liberals on your back who want to get tough on the causes of zombyism as well as on zombies. There are no NGO advocacy groups watching your moves, such as Zombie Rights Watch, Zombie Aid or Zombies without Frontiers (Drezner, 2011, 50). This is a war, in other words, that affords a clarity of purpose that no other struggle can, and of course the simplest rules of engagement: shoot on sight.

But remember this is all a fantasy; zombies are not real. The wars that you are likely to find yourselves fighting in your careers will involve ethical dilemmas not yet suspected. You'll have to worry about unintended consequences or what you euphemistically call 'collateral damage'. You'll have to wrestle with proportionality (the concept that the harm done in war should be in proportion to the good that can be expected from victory). You'll still have to take prisoners of war and apply the laws of war. Remember at the heart of every war is the relationship between our enemies and ourselves. It's our own mortality that is the root of our moral responsibility to others. Our first duty is ontological: to recognise that human responsibility matters because the idea of humanity matters. Indeed, it's only by relating to other people that we remain moral beings. If we choose not to relate to our enemies we will act immorally whether we consciously elect to do so or not.

CADET 4:   Awesome.

CLAUSEWITZ: Thank you.

INSTRUCTOR: Unfortunately, we have to wrap it up there, ladies and gentlemen. As you have discovered this afternoon the General is a great thinker. And what is a great thinker?

It's someone with the ability to ask questions in the right way, to step back and see the problems that we all face from a different angle of vision. The answers they provide are not so extraordinary that we are taken aback; what surprises us is that they're so obvious that we haven't come up with them before.

CLAUSEWITZ: And you shouldn't leave this seminar room with the idea that *On War* is the last word. By mid-century when you will be ending your careers a lot will have changed. Remember what scientists tell us—as knowledge expands, so our contact with the unknown grows as well. In short, we are always being confronted with the extent of our own ignorance.

3

WHAT IF CLAUSEWITZ HAD READ DARWIN?

In his book *The Sense of Style* Steven Pinker takes to task one of the great military historians of the recent past, John Keegan (Pinker, 2012). He acknowledges that his historical writing enriched our understanding of war, but he finds him very confused in his criticism of Clausewitz and his most famous dictum that war is the continuation of politics by other means. Take the passage in Keegan's *History of Warfare* in which he comments on discussion by 'the hapless Clausewitz' of the role of the Cossacks in the Tsar's army during the 1812 campaign (Keegan, 1993). Clausewitz was appalled by their cruelty—they would often strip French soldiers of their uniforms and leave them to die in subarctic temperatures, or sell them on to the serfs. But why should he have expressed surprise or even claim to have been shocked?

> Clausewitz was a man of his times, a child of the Enlightenment, a contemporary of the German Romantics, an intellectual, a practical reformer ... Had his mind been furnished with just one extra intellectual dimension ... he might have been able to perceive that war embraces much more than politics; that is also an expression of culture, often a determinant of cultural forms, in some societies the culture itself.

Pinker has much sport with this passage. Didn't Keegan also say earlier on that Clausewitz put too much stock in culture and too little on anthropology, and that he invested too much trust in the institutions, laws and prohibitions of the culture of his own age. Didn't he criticise him for making too little allowance for the endemic warfare of non-state, even pre-state, peoples in which there was no distinction between lawful and unlawful bearers of arms since all males were warriors? And what of psychoanalysis that 'seeks to persuade us that the savage in all of us lurks not far below the skin.' How then, can Clausewitz's problem be that he didn't put enough stock in culture? For that matter how can Clausewitz be both a product of the Enlightenment and of the German Romantic movement, which arose in reaction to the former? (Pinker, 2012, 181).

Pinker is right. Clausewitz's theoretical proposition that war is a continuation of politics is not hostile to culture: politics is actually its sub-text. But there is a problem with Clausewitz's theory. It may be illuminating but it is not illuminating enough. His objectives were at one and the same time too ambitious and too modest given his inadequate understanding of cultural anthropology. The brief historical *tour d'horizon* of war which he offers his readers in Book 8, for example, neither attempts to trace it back to its origins nor broadens out to offer any real insight into the future.

Let us remind ourselves of what Clausewitz tell us in what he modestly calls his 'passing glance at history' (*On War*, 8, 3b). The semi-barbarous Tatars searched for land; the ancient city-states limited their wars to plundering the countryside and seizing a few towns; a few empires arose, notably the Macedonian and Roman, that were able to consolidate their rule and extend their boundaries; the feudal kingdoms of medieval Europe could only assemble small armies based on vassalage and personal engagement—he notoriously dismissed them as of limited intellectual interest; 'once cattle had been driven off and castles burned they would go home.' The great commercial cities and republics of medieval Italy could afford mercenary armies who fixed battles for their own advantage: 'extremes of energy or exertion were conspicuous by their absence and fighting was generally a sham.' Then there appeared the first nation-states and the great wars between England and France in the fourteenth and fifteenth centuries that ended in the bid for French hegemony, beginning with the reign of Louis XIV and ending with Napoleon.

This single paragraph abridgement of Clausewitz's attempt to illustrate the changing character of war barely does justice to the five or six pages that he devotes to it; you will find a much longer discussion of the economic and social forces at work that predisposed societies to fight in ways consistent with their resources. But to be frank, Clausewitz's rundown has been challenged by historians and now is of little historical value. The nomads pioneered a way of warfare that was devastatingly effective: concentring force at critical points and combining speed with mass. The Mongols were particularly skilled at intelligence gathering—they were always better informed than their enemies, even about dissensions and quarrels within their opponents' ranks. Nor were Medieval armies the hicks that he made out; the Crusades, especially the early ones, involved an extraordinary logistic and financial effort (Tyerman, 2015). Fifteenth century mercenaries were highly competent and far ahead of anyone else in the latest military thinking. And eighteenth century armies, far from being preoccupied merely with 'points of detail', were perfectly au fait with what Clausewitz called 'the fundamentals of war.'

The real value of Clausewitz's historical *tour d'horizon* is his insight that every age has its own way of warfare—'its own limiting conditions and peculiar preconceptions.' And every historical period has its own theory of war—an understanding of what it is about, and why it is waged. This critical insight has now entered general understanding. In a recent book on the Afghan way of war the author is at pains to inform the reader that the four Afghan wars which the British have fought since 1839 allow us to come to three general conclusions. Afghans don't 'win' their wars on the battlefield; they usually co-opt unwilling foreigners to support one side against another and then dump them. The ISAF force which established itself in Kabul after the fall of the Taliban was cynically manipulated by a series of power brokers and warlords. Foreigners often complain about massacres and mutilation of prisoners but these reflect less a savage nature than a clever way of encouraging foreigners to depart after they have outstayed their welcome. But the central thesis of the study is that Afghans like everyone are pragmatic—they constantly experiment. They employed sharp shooters in the second Afghan war and improvised explosive devices (IEDs) in the most recent. It is the invaders who try to stereotype them by applying such catch-all labels as 'fanaticism' or 'religious fundamentalism'—the word Clausewitz would have privileged would have been 'savage' (Johnson, 2013).

Survival, however, is a competitive process. Competitive processes bring social life into being and allow it to thrive, at least for a time. Success and failure are 'designed' in by the stress of competition. Not only is competition perpetual; the rules of competition keep changing all the time. Societies pioneer a way of warfare which reflects their social and economic life; sometimes it wins over every other thanks to a superior technology (the longbow or machine gun) or a different, more ruthless understanding of war. And evolution explains everything about war, as it does about life—its complexity and diversity. The extraordinary success of the theory owes much to its elegance or what scientists understand by the term: the power to explain so much while assuming so little.

Evolution

You might well wonder then, writes Susan Blackmore, why, if the idea of evolution by means of natural selection is so powerful, no-one had thought of it before Darwin. The reason, she suspects, is that because there seems to be a tautology at its heart. 'Things that survive, survive'; 'successful ideas are successful'. To turn those tautologies into power you need to grasp that not everything survives, that competition is the name of the game and that in an ever-changing world the rules of competition keep changing, too. Copy the survivors many times with slight variations and let them loose in an ever-shifting world and only those suited to the new conditions will thrive (Blackmore, 2013, 1). It's the simplicity of this idea that accounts for its attractiveness beyond the world of biology.

Several contemporary writers have applied Darwin's ideas beyond the natural world. Two recent examples are Mark Sumner's *The Evolution of Everything: How Selection Shapes Culture, Commerce and Nature* (Sumner, 2010) and Matt Ridley's *The Evolution of Everything: How New Ideas Emerge* (Ridley, 2015). Both writers employ the idea figuratively, of course, to describe unfolding or emergent behaviour, but they are Darwinian in arguing that evolution as a conceptual device allows us to piece together the different characteristics of any human activity into a coherent whole. What makes the theory so radical is that it changes our way of thinking. It predisposes us to see cumulative change from very simple beginnings; it implies that change comes from within rather than being 'programmed' from without; it tells us that there is no blue-print or grand design or 'hidden hand'. Everything unfolds from the bottom up. Things never stay the same; they change gradually but inexorably; they show 'path dependence' and 'descent with modification'; they show 'selective' persistence. The idea has since spread to almost every field of life on the understanding, first articulated by one of Clausewitz's contemporaries, the Scottish Enlightenment thinker Adam Ferguson, that the world may be one of human action but not necessarily human design (Ridley, 2015, 4).

To reduce the concept to its essentials we might say that evolution shows how cumulative complexity emerges over time, fitting form to function. War and language are very similar. Both evolve by the selective survival of sequences generated by at least partly random variations. Both are combinatorial systems capable of generating diversity from a small number of elements. In the case of both the end result is structure and rules of grammar. Both are driven by a 'logic' which makes them 'rules-based.' Ways of warfare of the kind Clausewitz discusses in his brief *tour d'horizon* proliferate over time and are moulded in turn by cultural selection. Very few now survive—the Apache, Maori, Zulu and samurai have all gone, as have most of the world's languages. And as it becomes more and more complex, war no longer pays such high dividends on belief. Yet within the societies that are still in the war business—like the US, China and Russia—war continues to evolve in new domains such as space and cyberspace. This development is another example of how evolution powers specialisation, and specialisation, in turn, powers innovation.

Let me add a caveat here: there is no direct comparison with biological evolution. Natural selection involves the competition of genes determined by an organism's environment. The changes or mutations that power the culture of war, such as new inventions or bright ideas are consciously directed. Secondly, DNA mutations are random and indifferent to whether they will improve an organism's 'fitness of purpose.' Indeed many are positively harmful. But what is especially attractive about the metaphor in both cases is the fact that it is non-teleological. It has nothing to say about 'direction' or 'Progress' in history. Indeed, it requires you to largely reject the meta-narratives spun by Clausewitz's contemporaries such as Kant who argued that as war got more destructive, so governments would come together and outlaw it (not within the existing international order, of course, but thanks to a new one); or Hegel, who thought that war was 'characterised as something which ought to pass away.' (Avineri, 1996, 136). What both writers did, in other words, is to ask a question Clausewitz refused to. If the character of war is constantly changing, what are the limits of those changes; will war ever reach a point where it abolishes itself? I think Clausewitz would have been much more attuned to the Darwinian idea that war will end only after it had exhausted its evolutionary possibilities.

And I think what he might have liked most about the evolutionary metaphor is that it continues to generate intense debate amongst evolutionists themselves. Thus, there is no general agreement on gradualism. Scientists like Stephen Gould have put forward ideas such as punctuated equilibria—sometimes we see rapid changes, and sometimes we don't. In the case of war, sometimes we see revolutions in military affairs (eleven have been identified so far in the Western world alone) although not everyone agrees that such revolutions are quite as frequent as claimed or even particularly revolutionary.

Had Clausewitz been familiar with Darwin's big idea I think he might even have modified his views about the radical change in the character of war heralded by the French revolution, or the dramatic new thinking behind Napoleon's way of waging it. Many of the so-called 'revolutionary' changes in organisation had been introduced before 1789 and much of the 'radical' new thinking was done in the 1760s and 1770s by writers whose names have largely disappeared from the history books and are known, if at all, only to professional historians. The point is that most change is incremental, powered by trial and error with innovation driven by recombination.

I think that Walter Bryce Gallie was absolutely right to postulate that everything might have been different if Clausewitz had read Darwin. Remember, the book came out 36 years after his death. Remember, too, that the concept, though one of the most radical ever to change our understanding of our own humanity, became accepted within a remarkably short time. The question is not whether Clausewitz would have embraced Darwinism (I think he almost certainly would), but whether he would have embraced Social Darwinism, which became very popular in military circles and especially in Germany in the run-up to the First World War. In her book *Reading Clausewitz* Beatrice Heuser admits that there are passages which taken in the context of German nationalism later in the nineteenth century did indeed lend themselves to pseudo-Darwinian justifications for the militarisation of society and the glorification of war (Heuser, 2002, 51). Clausewitz was an ardent nationalist, even for his age. Reading him at times reminds us that towards the end of the nineteenth century nationalism became for many a surrogate religion. Like God, the nation became one, sacred, autonomous, self-grounding, without end or origin, a source of eternal life, deserving of veneration and, of course, sacrifice.

Let me just add one further observation: Clausewitz also laboured under two other handicaps. One was that although he can be said to have 'pioneered' the professional study of military history at military academies, history as an academic discipline had yet to be invented. Until then, as with Gibbon's great study of the decline and fall of the Roman Empire, history was used for a variety of ends. In Gibbon's case, as a prompt for moral reflection. And anthropology too had yet to witness its academic 'uplift' though there were great anthropologists already working away in the field. Perhaps, one of the reasons why Clausewitz was so impressed by the 'mysteries of war' is that many of the intellectual tools that have permitted some degree of demystification had not yet been invented.

Revisiting Clausewitz's phenomenology of war

Let me stick out my neck further still. Were Clausewitz alive today he might have been drawn to the framework for understanding animal behaviour that was put forward by the Dutch ethologist, Nikolass Tinbergen. Tinbergen, who was awarded the Nobel Prize in Physiology in 1973, formulated four questions to explain animal behaviour. He derived them from Aristotle's four causes of things, two of which are proximate and two ultimate, but you don't have to know that to appreciate their elegance of design. Think of them as the scaffolding upon which to build our own answers to what Clausewitz called the 'mystery' of war:

> *What are its origins? How did it first arise?*
> *What is its development (or mechanism): what are the changes that were necessary*

for it to flourish?
What is its ontogeny, its historical evolution across time?
What is its function, its adaptive significance (i.e., the role of behaviour in
facilitating reproductive success)? (Pepperberg, 2013, 383)

These are the questions that every phenomenologist of war should ask, and we ask them because we are Darwinists to the core even if we have never read a word of his work. Clausewitz wasn't and that is a major limitation of his work.

Origins

'I sing of ants and the man,' writes the Harvard socio-biologist E. O. Wilson in a novel about the world's two dominant species. He is echoing the opening lines of Virgil's epic poem, *The Aeneid* (Wilson, 2011, 1). But ants don't really lend themselves to epic poetry, do they? And even if you are a socio-biologist the fact that we have poetry and they don't surely makes all the difference? Wilson is being provocative, of course, in claiming that evolutionary selection and gene expression set limits on the influence that culture has on human behaviour. It is summed up in his famous claim that 'cognition will be translated into circuitry' (Wilson, 1980). It was the biologist Stephen J. Gould who challenged that argument:

> Genes make enzymes and enzymes control the rates of chemical pro-
> cesses. Genes do not make 'novelty seeking' or any other complex and
> overt behaviour. Predisposition via a long chain of complex chemical reac-
> tions, mediated through a more complex series of life circumstances, does
> not equal identification or even causation (Gould, 2001, 282).

Since Darwin we have been asking ourselves whether war is more genetic than cultural. The smart money tends to be on the latter. Culture, in other words, appears to be the key. We have it, ants don't.

Add to this the fact that ants are also biologically different from us. They are all related to each other—the warriors are female off-spring of a central queen. Sharing three-quarters of their genes with their sisters they readily sacrifice for the group; it is their best chance to perpetuate their own genes: 'Death in battle is trivial compared with an army made up of genetic near-replicates.' (O'Connell, 1996, 346). Although it is the oldest members, the grandmothers, who do most of the fighting, ants are nothing if not pragmatic. The US Marines boast that they never leave a man down; ants don't either: they eat their wounded. Not much that is poetic about that, is there?

Primatologists tell us that chimpanzees engage in war, too. But we must be careful not to chimpamorphise *Homo sapiens* and its ancestors. What is interesting is that there would seem to be only one area in which we have a physical advantage over chimpanzees; we can throw much better than they can, whether the object in question is a stone or a spear (an advantage that offsets our inadequacy in meeting the animals that once preyed upon us face to face). We can also out-think them, thanks to language and culture, both of which would appear to be evolutionary compensations for our physical feebleness (Fernandez-Armesto, 2005, 54).

Of course chimps may have basic Machiavellian intelligence—they can form alignments and work together. *Chimpanzee Politics* is the title of a book by the world's most famous primatologist, Frans De Waal (De Waal, 1982/2007). The real difference between us and our nearest cousins, however, is to be found in our brains. In his book *The Prehistory of the Mind*, Steven Mithen contends that critical step in the evolution of the human mind—the one we have today—was the move from a specialized to a generalised type of mentality (Mithen, 1998). We evolved to be pattern-seeking, causation-finding individuals. Those who were good at seeing patterns—the months when animals breed, or when in the course of the day they go down to the watering hole— were good at hunting, and left behind more offspring. The trick, of course, is to identify the right patterns of behaviour, and not the wrong ones. You may mistake a group of people associating together to see the sun going down for a group that is massing in preparation for an attack, at which point you are in grave danger of falling into the famous Hobbesian trap—attacking first before you are attacked.

In other words, our brains have evolved shared conceptual frameworks, emotional programmes and content-specific reasoning procedures 'that operate beneath the surface of expressed cultural variability and whose designs constitute a precise definition of human nature.' (Shermer, 2002, xxiii). What our Stone Age minds afford us is superior reasoning abilities; we can reason out what is good for us (peace); we can also reason out what is bad for us (war). Unfortunately, our rationality is 'bounded'. Cognitive dissonance, confirmation bias and premature cognitive closure are all human traits.

Clausewitz had nothing to say about any of this because he knew nothing about such matters, any more than did any of his contemporaries. He tells us only one thing. It is his big idea that was probably derived from Montesquieu: war proper began not from occasional marauding or from ordinary aggression, but when the 'weak defender' hit on the idea of organised resistance. But I think he would have been interested in the argument outlined in the preceding paragraphs. For the complexity of war that fascinated him so much inheres only in part in our biology; it also inheres in the role that cultural evolution plays in the awakening of human faculties that often gives the the weaker party an advantage of having to outthink the stronger (Midgley, 1995, 145). We strive to outperform so that we will be remembered: Alexander wept when he was told by the philosopher Anaxarchus that there were parallel universes out there; he wanted to conquer not only his own world but others. He succeeded anyway in writing himself into the history books. Our ambition to use every faculty is what led us to out-distance our nearest cousins.

Mechanisms

If Clausewitz has almost nothing to say about the origins of war, he also had remarkably little to say about its mechanisms. In physics we have developed several mental concepts to explain the mechanisms through which nature acts: such as mass, energy, force, velocity and momentum. Of these force (or interaction) is perhaps the most central to our understanding of the physical world. And when we turn to biology we find that genes recombine thanks to sexual activity to produce biological novelty. Organisms are merely vehicles used to perpetuate effectively immortal digital sequences written in DNA.

So, what are the cultural mechanisms through which war actually works?

Clausewitz is silent on these matters; his work makes little or no reference to the arts. There is no mention of Homer, or the pictorial representation of conflict. Perhaps like Robert E. Lee he would have thought the novel had nothing to say to a general. The greatest novel about war, *War and Peace* had yet to be written. It is interesting though to speculate what Clausewitz might have made of the Russian author's ruminations on the force of history and Napoleon's role in events. Even if he might not have warmed to the novel's characters he might still have engaged with its philosophical arguments.

Literature is important for a reason. In her book *Blood Rites* Barbara Ehrenreich reaches the conclusion that war is contagious. It spreads from one culture to the next thanks to epic poetry, the movies, and most recently computer gaming. Literature has an especially adaptive function—it provides us with role models, and inspiring tales of adventure, and tells us that there is a life out there to be lived on a higher emotional register than we can find at home. War embodies if you like a loose assemblage of algorithms or programs (in the computer sense of the term) for collective action. The idea that it is glorious to die for one's country has persisted for centuries. In that respect culture cannot always be counted upon 'to be on our side'. 'In so far as it allows humans to escape the imperatives of biology, it may do so only to entrap us in what are often crueller imperatives of its own' (Ehrenreich, 1997, 235).

Ehrenreich thinks of war as a 'meme'—a term introduced by Richard Dawkins back in 1976 and which is defined by the *Oxford English Dictionary* as 'an element of culture that may be considered to be passed on by non-genetic means.' Memes are said to resemble genes in that they produce cultural change through a process similar to natural selection; they are passed on by imitation and learning. There is a raw struggle for survival going on out there and it is not between organisms but between 'meme constructs.' It is a controversial theory, and some historians insist that it pushes the human capacity for imitation too far, while others contend that it is not so much an explanation as a highly incomplete description of change (Corfield, 2007, 70). Nevertheless I still think it explains quite a lot.

The last 200 years have seen more than forty English language editions of *The Iliad* (eight so far this century), a veritable Stakhanovite level of production. An edition of another inspiring war classic, Shakespeare's play *Henry V* was issued to the US soldiers deployed in Afghanistan and Iraq. Both the Homeric heroes and the English king are thugs; so why do we admire them? Language. The poetry. As Nietzsche said of Homer, he 'spiritualised away the cruelty'. Language doesn't airbrush out the cruelty of war; it amplifies it, but it does so in an inspiring fashion. As the novelist Thomas Keneally argues in his own novel of the Second World War, *Shame and the Captives* (2014) 'fiction has always tried to tell the truth (about war) by telling lies—by fabrication.' (Keneally, 2014, vii).

Another mechanism—still using the evolutionary metaphor—is technology. Since the day we first used weapons we have been involved in a kind of cognitive arms race. In 1908 the French philosopher Alain put it in a poetical way: every boat is copied from another boat. A very badly made boat will end up at the bottom of the sea after one or two voyages and thus will never be copied. 'One could then say, with complete rigor, that it is the sea itself who fashions the boats, choosing those which function and destroying the others.' (Ridley, 2015, 128). What changes the balance in favour of some and against others is not what is new but what is functional. War has its own wants. It destroys superannuated technologies and promotes dynamic ones, and it is quite ruthless in rooting out redundant systems. Countries that try to ban new technologies pay a price: the Chinese forbidding the construction of ships with two masts that could cross oceans only to face British steamboats in their own waters 300 years later; the Japanese Shoguns banning the use of firearms only to meet up with Commodore Perry's gunboats in Tokyo Bay in 1853.

Clausewitz's phenomenological model of war is notoriously incomplete in many other ways, too as Gallie reminds us (Gallie, 1991, 61). Taking him to task, Keegan identified four material mechanisms of which you won't find any mention in the pages of *On War*.

Stimulants (drink / drugs) When you find yourself contending with the trauma of battle you may have recourse to one tried and trusted option: getting stoned or smashed. Homer tells us that the heroes took opium. Soldiers smoked marijuana in Vietnam. In Clausewitz's day alcohol was the preferred stimulant. Full barrels of spirits were rolled into the squares at Waterloo, which was not so much a battle, as a brutal slugfest, the ultimate test of steadiness under fire, with victory going to the side that could still commit fresh reserves. Today modern armies use stimulants sparingly because of their side-effects. Cut to the Korangal Valley in Afghanistan forty years later and you find an intensity of combat much greater than Vietnam. In Sebastian Junger's account of the fighting, written from the perspective of an embedded journalist, we see that war is just as lethal, but framed by a totally different environment. Soldiers today enhance their physical and mental strength through arduous training; they are also more disciplined and hedged in by rules of engagement than they were in the past. They do not use drugs so much as soft porn and heavy metal music to dull the senses. (Junger, 2011)

The situation on the other side of the hill is very different. When the War on Terror began American Marines were forced to change their operational tactics after they discovered that many of the insurgents they fought in the Second Battle of Fallujah (November–December 2004), were quite literally stoned. Amphetamines, cocaine and piles of hypodermic needles and syringes were found in houses used by the irregulars in Iraq (Perry, 2005). Autopsies performed on the fallen rebels of the Abu Musab al-Zarqawi group found that many had been equally 'high' at the time of their deaths. In the Mumbai attack (2008), psychoactive substances, particularly cocaine, made it possible for the terrorists to continue their fight against Indian Special Forces for 2.5 days without sleep, rest and little food (McElroy, 2008). The Russian Prosecutor General's Office confirmed that almost all the Chechen terrorists who seized the Russian school at Beslan in September 2004 were addicted to both heroin and morphine. Many of them were intoxicated during the assault. When in the course of the three day siege they ran out of supplies they began to suffer severe withdrawal effects that may have led to the massacring of the children at the very end. (Kamienski, 2016)

Coercion is another factor in war that finds no place in Clausewitz's book. Officers have always tried to keep men in check by threatening punishment if they break the rules. In Clausewitz's day a sergeant with a pike pushed behind the rear ranks. Cavalry blocked the line of retreat for the infantry. In the First World War, officers with guns in hand, policed the communications trenches and ensured the men really did go 'over the top'. At Stalingrad special Red Army units were used to machine-gun down deserters. Keegan refers to the role that coercion increasingly played in keeping men in the killing zone as war became more impersonalised and remote:

> It's a function of the impersonality of modern war that the soldier is coerced, certainly at times by people who he can identify, but more fre-

quently, more continuously, and more harshly, by vast, unlocalised forces against which he may rail, but at which he cannot strike back and to which he must ultimately submit: the fire which nails him to the ground or drives him beneath it, the great distance which yawns between him and safety, the onward progression of a vehicular advance or retreat which carries him with it, willy-nilly. (Keegan, 1976, 324).

And then there is reward: *loot*. Even in Clausewitz's day war was profitable. Frank McLynn reminds us that Napoleon's Italian campaign in 1796 was a 'gigantic raid' by which his soldiers were able to enrich themselves by looting whatever fell their way (McLynn, 1997). Napoleon himself was happy enough to loot galleries like the Uffizi in Florence (just before the campaign in northern Italy students from the French Academy were to be found snooping around with measuring tapes to make sure that the packing cases the French brought with them were the right size) (Broers, 2010, 53). Ivy Compton-Burnett once complained that most novels which are meant to represent life have far too much to say about sex and far too little about money. Clausewitz had too much to say about the nation-state and national glory and too little about the pecuniary arrangements that made both France and Napoleon himself very rich.

That element lost its main motivating force in western armies after the mid-nineteenth century largely because it was not there. The institution of awards for bravery, such as the Legion of Honour, the Victoria Cross and in the United States the Medal of Honor became a token substitute for loot (sometimes they came with a pension, though over time, honour replaced value or interest) (Keegan, 1997, 7).

Elsewhere in the world, however, loot is still one of the defining reasons why irregulars stick together. Warlords like Charles Taylor in Liberia are the great beneficiaries (as Napoleon and his generals were in 1796). The ordinary foot soldiers get their share, just as Japanese soldiers got their 'comfort women' in the Second World War. Here is one eye-witness account from Liberia from a refugee who saw how fighters resorted to excessive violence to enrich themselves: 'Death and humiliation puts the genuine adults and achievers into their shells. The vacuum is then filled in by the young ones ... for them chance (and not age, valuable time and energy) creates material wealth.' (Reno, 2009, 340).

Of all the four mechanisms of combat motivation discussed by Keegan, it is his last that I find of most interest. It was the example set by the Big Man, a term that he borrowed from Polynesian warrior society (Keegan, 1997, 8–11). State authorities may disapprove of mavericks and their comrades even dislike them, but they are the ones who, like Achilles, bring combat alive. They are the principal performers in what we still call a 'theatre' of war. They have the power of sporting heroes. And they encourage mimicry. They set the gold standard. They energise the raw material with which combat is conducted (Keegan, 1997, 10). Such men neither lead nor command. And they are also dangerous. Their violence can descend into frenzy; they can develop a love of killing. They can inspire precisely the wrong example. Not for them the set texts of Staff College curricula which Keegan (with his well-known disdain for Clausewitz) added might be the dead-end in the study of war.

In the fourth case we are dealing with the concept of agency. And the concept in turn often refers back to religion. In a book by the complexity theorist Stuart Kaufman we find an argument that value is a part of the language appropriate to the non-reducible real and emergent activities of agents (Kaufman, 2008). What motivates young men to go out to Syria and Iraq to join ISIS? What explains their combat motivation? 'Spiritual unemployment' and an 'impoverishment of the will and impulse'—the words are those of Van Wyck Brooks from his book *America's Coming of Age* (1915). Woodrow Wilson took his country to war two years later for the stated purpose of making the world 'safe for democracy', but it also offered a chance for America's spiritual regeneration, a rediscovery of its 'will and impulse'. Both would seem to have vanished from the western world, only to have been reborn on battlefields further afield. The imperative can be found in a letter that Saul Bellow wrote to a friend about his character Augie Marsh. Augie, he added, was the embodiment of the willingness to serve, a man who says, 'For God's sake, make use of me, only do not use me to no purpose'. Surely, Bellow added, the greatest human desire is to be used.

Ontogeny

Where Clausewitz scores is with regard to the last two items of Tinbergen's conceptual framework; he was much more interested in the ontogeny and the function of war. Clausewitz's idea of the changing character of war was derived from a comprehensive study of history. Today we might run with an evolutionary metaphor. Different styles of war—or ways of warfare—are a vivid example of 'descent with modification'. Evolution proceeds via branching through common descent—ways of warfare are similar but not exact replicas of what came before. It is this variation that allows for perpetual adaptation. And then there is the multiplication of speciation, that is, evolution produces an increasing number of new species. Such changes are rarely revolutionary; they are slow and steady. The same dynamic in war appears in different historical eras but operates differently according to the historical matrix in which it functions.

Perhaps, the most famous example of cultural adaptation is that of Japan. By the late sixteenth century the Japanese were the main gun manufacturers in the world. They had pioneered a serial firing technique that was not to be seen in Europe until sixty years later. So why did they choose to abandon guns some time later. There are a number of possible explanations; as usual historians cannot agree. One is that they found objectionable the equality that a gun-bearing peasant had with a samurai swordsman, and the samurai found even more objectionable the fact that the skill of engagement passed from the swordsman to the manufacturer of the gun. Another is that Japan faced no external competitors with guns and therefore had no need of an armaments industry. A third is that guns were not indigenous; they were imported, even though the Japanese adapted them and improved their design by inventing a helical mainspring and an adjustable trigger-pull. Once the Japanese decided to shut themselves off from the outside world, they also rejected any technology that was foreign (Hillsman, 2004, 162–6).

Fast-forward to the nineteenth century and we find in the United States a society that operated on very different lines. Shortly after Clausewitz's death two national armouries at Harpers Ferry and Springfield were established and built the first fully interchangeable firearms in the world. The standardisation of parts made possible the first mass arms production of weapons. Instead of industrialists offering the military a range of inventions the military set requirements and corporations struggled to meet them. Another constant in modern

American history is capitalism and its remarkable appetite for risk; time and again big business and the military gambled fistfuls of money on proofs of concepts. The result was the military-industrial complex. The US also pioneered very early on an engineering attitude to war: West Point was originally established as an engineering school. And later in the twentieth century it set up research hubs like the Defense Research Programme Agency. The result was that the US rapidly became the most innovative military power in history. (Whiteman, 2015)

Functions

It is when we come to the function of war that Clausewitz really comes through. War is principally determined, he tells us, not by ideas or inventions, but by social factors. (*On War*, 6, 30). Collective violence is the way by which societies accumulate power and direct it to certain instrumental and existential ends such as profit or honour. And what we understand to be war is not so much the ambushes and raids in which hunter-gatherer societies have engaged in for 90 per cent of human history, but the organised conflicts that arose with the invention of agriculture. We can trace a distinctive historical transition when human beings began to shift away from gathering food to producing it. Ken Binmore, a mathematician by training who broke new ground by bringing game theory to bear on questions of moral philosophy, argues that when the economic means of production change, so the social contract changes, too. We move from an egalitarian social contract to a hierarchical one. Private property appears and then the leaders to organise things and to protect the interests of the community. Chieftain societies were able to mobilise more human resources and direct war to more ambitious social goals such as theft or grand larceny (slave raiding) (Voorhoeve, 2009, 150).

Before that, however, warfare probably developed from hunting. Both required the same skills and the same tools, after all. In Aristotle's *Politics* we are told there are five main ways by which men live by their labour. There is the pastoral, agricultural and fishing, but the inclusion of hunting perhaps comes as a shock, and even more perhaps the fact that he divides it into several sub-themes: the hunting of wild animals, the hunting of people (slave raiding), the hunting of moveable objects (plundering) and the hunting of people and possessions together (war). The Greeks were not squeamish when it comes to spelling out reality.

Is the situation so different today? 'How do we organise the Defense Department for manhunts' Donald Rumsfeld asked at the beginning of the War on Terror, and some see drone warfare as man-hunting on a grand scale. Invoking Clausewitz's classic definition of war as a duel, Gregoire Chamayou writes that the fundamental structure of this type of warfare is not that of two fighters squaring off against each other, but that of a hunter advancing on his prey. And the profession of man-hunting now has its own technocratic jargon, he adds, derived in part from Social Network Analysis (SNA) and 'nexus-topography', a pseudo-science which enables us to map social forms or environments which bind individuals together and so allow us to identify the critical nodes in a network (and take them out). (Chamayou, 2015)

The point that anthropologists make is that different societies have different ways of understanding war, but they also have different ways of valuing it precisely because it fulfils different functions. 'There is no algorithm to determine what we should welcome or when we should be wary of systems of belief that differ radically from our own' (Lloyd, 2012, 117). There is no reason for concluding we know the 'truth' of war, even if it is there to be found. The truth, for that reason, is always provisional and it may be that some societies at this stage of the game have greater imaginative resourcefulness than we do.

Yet Beatrice Heuser is right to be critical of Clausewitz for not taking his thoughts further; for not really thinking hard about the future of war. He showed little interest in the French revolutionary ideas that might one day influence the political aims of war (Heuser, 2007, xix). He cannot be criticised, of course, for not foreseeing some of the ideologies that were to arise in the course of the century, such as racism and nationalism. (He died a year after the outbreak of the Greek revolt [1830] which turned out to be an early example of the ethnic cleansing for which the Balkans was to become especially well-known in the twentieth century. Almost 200,000 Turks were expelled or forced to flee).

By 1850 the battle lines of the future were beginning to take shape—nationalism was about to offer governments the chance to mobilise human capital on a scale that Napoleon would have envied. I think Clausewitz would have been amazed to have been told that in the

First World War the German state was able to call upon 86 per cent of the country's entire male population between the ages of 18–50 (Watson, 2014, 2).

And after the revolutions of 1848 race-based universal themes began to come to the fore. One of the striking features of such thinking, as Alexis de Tocqueville was one of the first to recognise, was its strong propensity to historical determinism (the belief in an inevitable racial fight to the death) and hence to the marginalisation of politics (and with it the idea of war as a 'continuation of politics by other means') (Osterhammel, 2014, 859). Hitler waged a race war in the East (a *Rassenkampf*), or a *Vernichtungskampf* ('a war of extermination'). 8.5 million Russian soldiers died, as well as 27 million civilians. What is remarkable about the Nazi way of warfare was that it was essentially apolitical—it had no realisable political end. 'Wherever our success ends,' wrote Hitler as early as 1928, 'it will always only be the point of departure for a new struggle.' As Telford Taylor adds, 'the downfall of the Third Reich was due in no small measure to Hitler's inability to realise that in strategic terms the road to everywhere is the road to nowhere.' (Jablonsky, 1994, 186).

So, what would Clausewitz have made of ISIS, or the Jihadists and suicide bombers who have become a familiar aspect of the political landscape of the Middle East? I suspect he might well have argued that their violence is largely functional; it works, and that's why we find it so threatening. Rodney Stark and William Banibridge, sociologists of religion, have pointed out that the more demanding a religion is, the more value it has for the devotee because of the sacrifices that have to be made, and that they think are worth making (Stark and Bainbridge, 1987). The point is that if you think in terms of Islam you will not get very far, but if you think in terms of the organisations that claim to represent it then you may have a better purchase on reality. Suicide bombers are like moths attracted to the flame. Their actions are good for religion and good for the group. They are good for religion in the abstract because those that die demand too little of themselves, not too much. They are good for the group in the same way that nucleated cells evolve into symbiotic communities of bacterial cells. What sociologists tell us about religion in general is that religious people are more pro-social than others. Usually they feel better about themselves, are less anxious about the future; they engage in more long-term planning than merely gratifying impulsive desires (Wilson, 2008, 129). A small cult becomes a global brand by suppressing selection within groups, making it difficult for selfish elements to evolve at the expense of other members of their own group. The concept is called 'major transition', the ability to acquire and socially transmit behaviour at the same time.

Of course, religions differ greatly and even within religions there is to be found a broad spectrum of views, from fundamentalism to liberalism, but nearly all of them are social (i.e., concerned with the definition of the social group and the regulation of social interaction within and between groups). From an evolutionary perspective what is important is survival and the propagation of the group—not so much 'good' behaviour or what the out-group (or even less other in-group members) might consider good. Boko Haram's leader may well think God is responsible for rain and that the Earth is flat and that young girls should be sold into slavery, but such thoughts, though grotesque, are not 'irrational' from an evolutionary perspective. Indeed these ideas make the group highly functional. Evolutionary theory, in other words, provides a powerful framework for studying terrorism and war as it does religion. Indeed there are many links between the two.

Clausewitz used the word 'grammar' only once but he used it for a purpose. War is a conversation. It is communicative. We convey our intentions through our actions. And of course we try to understand our enemies through their actions, through their language (the suicide bomber). And we assume because we have patented, in our eyes at least, a superior form of war which is more rational and even more humane, that once our message has been deciphered then they will reply in our code. Of course, the trick is to remember that our enemies are not pre-modern or pre-industrial. They are not so foreign that they really are from a distant galaxy (imagine trying to 'win the narrative' if we had engaged the Huns in the fifth century, or even more challenging the Mongols in the thirteenth). Armies have often the gene pool of the population through which they move, but the Mongols engaged in rape on such an extensive scale that according to an Oxford team of geneticists an unusual Y chromosome among Asian males can be traced back to Genghis Khan and his family. The Mongols, in other words, employed what was in effect a novel form of 'social selection' by changing patterns of variation in human DNA (Brookes, 2015, 31).

So very different from ISIS with its social media sites, and even the message which it conveys—part hipster cool, part consumerist. By comparison, there is an irreducible otherness about the Mongols which is why they still live on in our collective memory. Whatever ISIS may be, it is a product of the twenty-first century, not as some would have it, of the Middle Ages in disguise.

Was Clausewitz Eurocentric?

Clausewitz's understanding of war was far more profound than that of any of his contemporaries. 'The way to judge him is to try to walk all round him,' Henry James famously said of Balzac, 'on which we can see how remarkably far we have to go.' The same is true of the man we are discussing; it is the breadth of his enterprise that still amazes us. Clausewitz does fall short at times but he only claimed to offer his readers a 'preliminary concept of war' which was intended to cast light on the 'basic structure of theory' and thus to help them identify its major components (*On War*, 1, 1.28) In this he broke new ground.

But his critics must be taken seriously, too. An important charge against him is that he was Eurocentric. And there is I would insist really no denying it. What he offers us, inevitably, is an ultimately distorted account of the history of war cast in the image of western scholarship. Why is this problematic? Because even if you assume that others operate outside Western frames of reference, fighting and dying by different rules of logic, you still end up relying on Western concepts to understand them (Porter, 2009, 152)

His vocabulary of war, for example, was derived entirely from Greek and Latin models. Take the words 'army', 'military', 'strategy' and 'tactics', as well as the metaphors which he would have known in his youth: 'if you want peace, prepare for war', or 'live or die by the sword'. Clausewitz's obsession with winning a decisive battle also owed more than he probably knew to Greek thinking. In the *Philippic*, Demosthenes bemoans the fact that of all arts the Greeks had taken the art of war to a new level—decisiveness. And decisiveness required shock battle (Hanson, 2003, 93). That would not matter so much but for the fact that the decisive battles he discusses in his book are almost all European. You won't find any reference in *On War* to the battles that appear on ISIS audio chips: Badr and Uhud; Mutah and Hunayn; Qadisiya and Yarmuk; Balat ash-Shuhada and Nahawand. The first four took place during the last decade of the prophet Mohammed and thus are foundation stones of the Islamic faith. Nahawand and Qadisiya were two victories that brought Persia into the Islamic world; Yarmuk was the battle that broke Byzantine control of the Middle East in AD 636. Balat al-Shuhada refers to the Battle of Tours (also called the Battle of Poitiers) in 732 where the Frankish forces under Charles Martel repulsed a Muslim raiding party (not as the Europeans of Clausewitz's day liked to think, a Muslim invasion of Western Europe). Today films about the Battles of Yarmuk or Hattin, which saw an Arab force destroy a Crusader army, often get half a million YouTube views (Burke, 2015, 39). 'Remember Hattin!' is a cry still heard from those seeking to do to the West what Saladin did to the Crusader kingdom of Jerusalem in 1187.

But if Clausewitz is indeed guilty of Eurocentrism, he had a much more nuanced understanding of the Western way of war than the historian Victor Davis Hanson, who first popularised the term in his early book *The Western Way of War: Infantry Battle in Classical Greece* (Hanson, 1989). Looking back to the ancient Greeks, he argues that the West has aimed for decisiveness on the battlefield. John Keegan took this argument further in his *History of Warfare*, in which he suggested that it reflected the principal of decisiveness in Greek life: in the theatre (the idea of catharsis); in mathematics (the Euclidian proof, absent from Indian mathematics, for example); in the law courts (the decisive argument that sways a jury). And both men thought the manner of fighting basic to the theory: shock battle had enabled smaller European armies to defeat much larger Asian ones (Keegan, 1993).

On the positive side of the ledger, Clausewitz does insist that the Western way of war is not unchanging; it is subject to frequent changes in style. Where Hanson stresses continuity in terms of the application of science, capitalism, individualism and what he calls civic militarism (with a healthy dose of anti-militarism thrown in to prevent Western societies from loving it too much), Clausewitz insisted that not only did the French and Germans think about war differently in his own day, both nations also broke with much of the conventional thinking of the mid-eighteenth century. And that is all the more interesting because some of the elements of Hanson's thesis reappeared in Clausewitz's day: the return of civic militarism in the form of the *levée en masse*; the decisive battles of Austerlitz and Jena; and the discipline of Napoleon's armies that allowed a remnant to make it back from Russia. But Clausewitz did not see fit to identify this with a long tradition of Western arms, any more than did Machiavelli in *The Art of War*, a book that may have inspired Clausewitz more than he was willing to acknowledge.

So Clausewitz's approach to military history did not postulate an unchanging Western way of war. None of which is gainsay the fact that a Western style had clearly emerged by the early nineteenth century. In the seventeenth century European armies marched in step; Turkish armies didn't. The West encouraged a division of labour that narrowed the range of skills. Soldiers focused on a specific skill set; they were taught to focus exclusively on what they knew best. This was not always an advantage. Disciplinary specialisation carried the risk that rigour might degenerate into rigidity, as was the case with the Prussian army after 1780 (Toulmin, 2001, 46). The need to strike a balance between rigidity and openness, to distinguish between the core values of discipline and the situations in which it applied, was all-important. That was the importance of the Prussian military reforms that were pioneered by Clausewitz's great mentor Scharnhorst and that laid the foundations for Prussia's eventual victory over Napoleon a few years later.

So in so far as the Western way of war is real, we should acknowledge two factors. The Western way was not superior to the non-western until the mid-nineteenth century, and owed much to industrialisation and the systematic application of science and technology to war-making which is also of comparatively recent vintage. And the advantage may not persist much longer. We should perhaps take note of the warning of Andrew Bacevich that our enemies have finally found the answer to the Western way of war (Bacevich, 2006).

Losing small wars

So Clausewitz was inescapably Eurocentric, but it doesn't follow that his work has nothing to say about the conflicts and confusions of our own age. One of the many criticisms levelled against him is that he has little to say about the wars we now fight against insurgents, jihadists, terrorists, or other politically motivated non-state actors. In fact he was one of the very first theorists of national liberation wars. Read his 'Lectures on Small Wars', which he delivered at the War School in Berlin in 1811–12 or the famous 1812 Memorandum in which he looked forward to a war of liberation in Germany itself. Or read the chapter on 'The People in Arms' in the sixth book of *On War*. These have been brought together by Christopher Daase and James Davis (Daase and Davis, 2015). At one time it was thought that had he lived Clausewitz would have brought out a companion volume on guerrilla warfare, though many historians now doubt this.

Unfortunately, the small wars of his day are not much remembered by students. They are a part of a history that is at once totally obscure and at the same time broadly familiar because they took place against the backdrop of the great battles students have heard of. Of all Napoleon's 'other wars' the most significant was the insurgency in Spain. When we compare it with America's experience in Iraq (2003–9) the parallels are both disturbing and illuminating. To begin with, historians have begun to see the Spanish insurrection as Europe's first religious war since 1648. An English observer at the time attributed the reluctance of the Spanish to surrender to the fact that their priests persuaded them to continue the fight to the bitter end: 'processions, miracles, prophecies, as well as the distribution of relics and the appointment of saints to the command of armies fanaticised the mass of patriots' (Haythornthwaite, 1996, 119). In this most terrible of conflicts the Enlightenment encountered an age people thought had been consigned to history. Other historians take a different view and see the insurrection as no more than 'tax-resistant brigandage' (McLynn, 1997, 454). With its ethos of xenophobia and taste for atrocity it left a baleful legacy that some say would eventually resurface in the Spanish Civil War a hundred years later (Broers, 2010, 106).

Napoleon, of course, knew what a bandit was, and he knew the difference between a bandit and a freedom fighter (his own father had been one of the latter). Banditry and guerrilla warfare were bound together from their inception. In Corsica and in Spain they were joined at the hip. As Charles Esdaile writes, honour killings and the culture of the vendetta were held in as high esteem as patriotism, and patriotism was often just a means of revenging the dead by proxy (Esdaile, 2004,

100–101), And French intervention, not only in Spain but in the Balkans and Italy, created opportunities for social outsiders that had not existed before (Broers, 2010, 17). Napoleon's 'little wars' saw pig farmers become Balkan princes, mule drivers become presidents of new countries, peasants' sons dictators of new provinces, and priests Mafia-style local bosses. Today, similar opportunities enable people to become self-appointed caliphs.

Even the manner in which the French attempted to retain control of the Spanish peninsula conjures up the urban battles the American army fought in Iraq. The insurrection in Madrid was repressed with French cavalry killing protestors one by one, street by street. In Saragossa there was house-to-house fighting. The city was first levelled by artillery, then fire-bombed before the soldiers moved in, bayonets fixed, shooting everyone on sight. In Iraq the two battles of Fallujah (2004) produced similar scenes, updated with modern technology. And just as the French found they had to conquer the Peninsula from the inside-out so the Americans were in danger of finding themselves in the same predicament in Iraq. As in Iraq, the insurgents attacked convoys, using swarming tactics in Navarre and Aragon, and engaging in atrocities (often directed by the priests) which sickened the French occupiers. Captured French soldiers routinely had their eyes gouged out by women wielding scissors, knitting needles and kitchen knives.

Even the Surge (2007) in Iraq had its counter-point in Spain when in 1810 the French pushed into Andalusia and took Seville. It was even successful for a while. Just as the Americans were able to utilise Sunni tribes, so the French army was able to utilise locals against the *partidas*—the criminals, who continued raiding into the countryside as late as 1816, two years after the fighting had officially ended. The French almost broke the back of the Insurgency in 1810–11, though they ultimately failed. The guerrillas on their own may not have won the war but they may have made Spain ungovernable for much of the nineteenth century. Deep-rooted criminality had been bred-in to such an extent that Spain became the most unstable country in Western Europe. The same, alas, may be true of Iraq—it may remain broken for years to come.

So what can be said of Clausewitz's overall view of insurgency? First and foremost he never questioned whether these 'small wars' were wars. He didn't take upon himself the role of modern commentators who in calling such conflicts 'new' (Kaldor) or 'degenerate' (Mueller) like to legislate what counts as knowledge, a phenomenon we see at work every time psychiatrists discover a new 'disorder' hitherto unknown, which allows them to pathologise what is really just a part of life. War is still war even when fought in peripheral areas. Indeed, the small wars of Clausewitz's day were so lethal precisely because they were peripheral to the main action. As Broers writes, the real point about the Vendée revolt (the Royalist attempted counter-revolution in the 1790s about which Clausewitz also wrote) was that it seemed to come out of nowhere and that was because the Vendée was nowhere in particular. It was a backwater, even by the standards of the time (Broers, 2010, 24).

Secondly, he did not allow himself to be traduced by language. The French Revolutionary era was the first when it was possible to condemn enemies for being 'counter-revolutionary' or 'un-progressive,' fighting the wrong historical corner. Revolution gave it the moral high ground from which to condemn any attempt at resistance as 'criminal', 'wayward', 'anarchical', 'degenerate', not war but something smaller in scale, more trivial (if still deadly). These days we tend to fall into the similar trap of condemning our enemies as 'barbaric', 'medieval,' 'anachronistic', or 'pre-modern'. And we often think that the wars we fight are 'new' when they are really not. By providing a theoretical underpinning for small wars, Clausewitz was able to underscore the fact that the Spanish insurrection was certainly a war.

He recognised very early on the critical importance of the insurrectionary conflicts that tied down so many of Napoleon's forces. His greatest insight was that the longer an external power fights the more likely it will confront a strategic endgame; the longer a guerrilla force fights the stronger it will probably become. Different criteria apply to the offensive and the defensive. Henry Kissinger summarised this insight in a single sentence: 'the guerrilla wins if he does not lose; the conventional army loses if it does not win.'

As Christopher Daase adds, Clausewitz is also quite insightful on the role of terror in such conflicts. What he didn't realise was that though terror begets terror, the terror of the insurgent is really a feature of the struggle itself. Occupying forces tend to see themselves as civilised and rule-bound even when they break the rules; non-state actors fighting strategically on the defensive but tactically on the offensive have no incentive to wage war according to any rules. This was the situation in the global war on terror—a small war writ large (Daase, 2005).

It was Clausewitz's greatest twentieth century interpreter, Raymond Aron, who came up with a term that I think is more useful than any other: 'polymorphous' (Aron, 1983). What he found in Algeria in the 1950s was a war that morphed from a war of liberation into a conflict which involved a large criminal element. Like a computer virus the insurgency in Algeria took many forms which proliferated over time. We are told that in the first twelve minutes that Microsoft software is switched on, computers now have a 50 per cent chance of catching a virus. Some leap from user to user and then lie dormant for months. Some evade immediate detection only to pop up later. Some are even programmed to undergo evolutionary mutations that their programmers cannot predict. Their importance is that they have no function other than their own reproduction. Most important of all, to employ a Darwinian term, there is no necessary connection between their own fitness—from their own reproductive point of view—and their contribution to the general fitness.

In his own book *The Utility of Force* Rupert Smith prefers the word 'rhizomatic' to describe how insurgency propagates like weeds by the roots below ground, swiftly and unseen (Smith, 2005). Smith had personal experience at the highest level both as a Divisional Commander in the First Gulf War and a UN Commander in Bosnia. What he found in Bosnia was that the conflict was not between peoples, or even ethnic groups, but ambitious politicians and their 'homeboy sub-contractors' (the phrase was coined by the anthropologist Clifford Geertz) who killed in the name of political leaders such as Milosevic, Karadzic and Tudjman, the politicians who did well, and their warlord allies who emerged from the detritus of Tito's Yugoslavia. And it was those private armies, eighty-three in all, that carried out murders for profit. Cruel when winning, they rarely put up much of a fight when losing. But they were rarely taken on. Unfortunately the nations that contributed to the UN force that he commanded had no intention of committing their soldiers to battle, or indeed of putting them at any risk. And because its members had such an imperfect understanding of the nature of the conflict, they frightened themselves into inaction.

Today, by contrast, some conflicts go far beyond what we witnessed in the 1990s in the Balkans, as did the national liberation struggles of the Cold War years. What would Clausewitz have made of them? It is a confusing picture because the general was both much more radical than his admirers often suspect, and not radical enough. Carl Schmitt took him to task for being so tied to classical categories such as the famous trinity, never grasping the fact that most partisan wars are non-trinitarian, as Martin van Creveld argued back in 1991. Why? Perhaps because the open-ended nature of partisan warfare offended his sense of order (Schmitt, 1962/2004). But that is a gross misrepresentation of his work. From the time he wrote to Fichte in 1809 complaining about the limitations of Machiavelli's understanding of warfare to the lectures he gave a few years later on low-intensity conflict, Clausewitz grasped that he was witnessing a new phenomenon—a further stage in the evolution of war. Some of these low-intensity conflicts had awakened popular sentiment. If not quite national liberation wars, they were certainly their precursors in which passions once unlocked were hard to contain.

Napoleon himself recognised that his forces in Spain had been forced to return to an earlier 'barbaric' phase of war. His leading commander General Lefebvre insisted: 'you have to fight like a partisan whenever there are partisans to fight.' (Schmitt, 1962/2004, 9). He and his subordinate commanders were confronted with the kind of war none of them wanted to fight: a manpower-intensive, drawn-out struggle of indeterminate length in which high-end technology was not dominant and encounters with the enemy were rarely decisive. Clausewitz's openly expressed enthusiasm for this kind of warfare (together with his attempt in 1813 to rouse the German nation and his role in organising basic insurgent forces against the French in the Baltic) inevitably awakened suspicions of his radicalism at the same time. He was to pay for this by being constantly passed over for higher command. He was not radical enough, however, in recognising that violence might one day be deliberately used by partisans (as in Algeria in the 1950s) to mobilise popular consciousness, to kick-start the people into revolution along the lines George Sorel advocated in the early years of the twentieth century.

And I suspect that Clausewitz might have found himself utterly confounded by much of the violence of our world which is directed almost exclusively against civilians. If you look at the German text of *On War* you won't find a single reference to *Zivilist* or *Zivilperson* (civilian). The reason could be that he later reintegrated guerrilla warfare into the general defence of the state; the people become an actor in someone else's story, not their own. Even in his ideal type of absolute war the carnage is largely focussed on the battlefield where there are no civilians. It is pretty likely that many of tomorrow's wars will probably privilege the role of non-state actors and be fought within cities without definable battlegrounds. I also suspect that Clausewitz would have been surprised to find that today's weapons of choice today are David's not Goliath's—the simple sling against the massively over-equipped Philistine warrior with his Bronze Age armour weighing in at nearly ten stone. What would he have made of Palestinian adolescents in the second intifada throwing stones against Israeli Markava tanks; or Hizbullah operatives firing rockets with an explosive warhead of only 2–5kg (over 10,000 of them) in the 2006 war against Israel; or the IEDs the Taliban employed with devastating effectiveness against heavily armed NATO forces? What all this may portend is something that Clausewitz would have found totally surprising; a change in the ownership of war. In other words, writes Aaron Karp, asymmetric warfare may no longer be 'a secondary face of armed conflict but the inevitable and increasingly dominant manifestation of its core meaning.' (Karp, 2009, 291).

Conclusion

Is it possible to say more? Of course it is and many other writers have done so. Clausewitzian scholarship is a constant work in progress. But I think I will close this chapter on a final note. Clausewitz's great book is of course a classic. 'The classics are those books which you usually hear people saying "I'm re-reading" ... never "I'm reading".' The observation is Italo Calvino's and the implication is that most usually go unread. But the word 'classic' also suggests that for those who actually bother to make the effort to read one, their understanding of life will be much amplified. And in re-reading a great work we may find what we did not find before.

Even when Clausewitz reached too far, wrote too much or revised too little he remained in touch with the complexity of war and asked all the right questions. Had he been acquainted with Darwin he might have asked different questions about war's idiopathic nature (the constant inter-changeability of functions/mechanisms that sustain it). But we can reboot *On War* by re-reading it through a new prism (in this case Darwinism). Such a process may involve some distortion but the distortion, I would argue, is far more of our preconceived ideas about war than Clausewitz's own understanding of it. He offers us a phenomenology which we have been defining, redefining and reshaping ever since in the light of our deepening knowledge of history and science. In 'rebooting' his work his true greatness as a writer can be not only recognised but also more fully understood.

4

AN EVENING DISCUSSION AT THE CENTER FOR THE AMERICAN CENTURY AFTER NEXT, WASHINGTON, D.C.

CLAUSEWITZ AND THE IMPORTANCE OF STRATEGY

Clausewitz finds himself on an evening panel discussion at the Center for the American Century After Next. It is a new think-tank in Washington DC, decidedly centrist—unusual in a town that does not do centre. 'The Center Can Still Hold' is its stirring motto. His fellow panellists are the scholar in residence Bill Lowry, author of the book After Baghdad, Beijing: The Follies of Neo-Conservatism; *and a 3-star US Marine Corps General who retired from active service after his third tour in Afghanistan. The subject tonight is 'The GlobalWar on Terror: Reflections and Lessons'. The moderator is the Pentagon correspondent for the* Washington Post.

MODERATOR: Good evening, ladies and gentlemen. We have a very special guest with us tonight, General Carl von Clausewitz. On the name recognition stakes he is up there with the greats. You may not have read his book, but you certainly know of him. So, if I were to say he needs no introduction, I'd be guilty of serious understatement. We are also fortunate to have General Alexander, a former 3-star Marine who was in the

93

Global War on Terror from the beginning and is a noted critic of the Bush years. He has been in the field and knows what war is (which is more than can be said for the politicians who took us into Iraq in 2003).

LOWRY: Was that a war? I thought it was a Republican Party commercial.

MODERATOR: Good one, Bill. But you stole it, you know, from a film, *The Last Supper*.

LOWRY: Yep, but that was about the First Gulf War, the one we won—kind of.

MODERATOR: Well ladies and gentlemen, Bill Lowry has just introduced himself. He is quite a wag! He is the Center scholar in residence and writes occasionally for my own paper, *The Post*. He has been an embedded journalist several times in his career, most recently with an Infantry unit in Afghanistan. You probably know him from his book *After Baghdad, Beijing*—a bestseller a few years back. What you may not know is that the title refers to a popular slogan in neo-conservative circles after Saddam was ousted. Well, it didn't happen of course. The Chinese got lucky.

What we're going to discuss tonight is what went wrong in Iraq and Afghanistan. We all have our opinions, I know, but they're not always well-informed. We have three experts on the panel, including the man who practically invented strategy as an academic subject. But I think, General Clausewitz, that you'd agree no-one really knows what strategy is?

CLAUSEWITZ: Well, they certainly don't seem to practice it today.

MODERATOR: Got you! Perhaps you've heard of Britney Spears?

CLAUSEWITZ: Britney? Is that a Christian name?

MODERATOR: Not sure about the Christian. We're a little more inventive when it comes to first names than in your day. But to cut to the chase: she is a pop—popular—singer.

CLAUSEWITZ: A *chanteuse?*

MODERATOR: Well, you might say that; I couldn't possibly comment. Anyway, she's a little erratic in her behaviour. One day she shaved her head. The following day her manager was asked whether she'd acted on impulse, or whether she'd been thinking about it for some time. 'Let's get one thing straight', he replied, 'Britney doesn't do strategy'.

Well, our world is far more complex than yours, I think it's fair to say, and we engage in different types of strategic thinking. We have life-strategies, for example. We have life-mentoring and life-coaching, all very American fads that date back to the 1930s. And then there are organisational strategies which you find taught in business school. We can date the beginning of organisational strategy back to the publication of a book by Alfred Chandler, *Strategy and Structure* (Chandler, 1962). Today's business consultants are two a dozen. The great attraction of business consultants is that you can send a team from the outside with no particular knowledge of the business in question; they'll analyse the data for you and write reports and make sure they drop the invoice before they leave (Qureshi, 2015). Some American business theorists believe that success is simply the result of (successfully) managing failure. They believe that failure contains 'tremendous growth energy'!

LOWRY: You may be interested to know, General, that the Boston Consulting Group, not normally known for having an overly philosophical approach to business, compiled a 'best of Clausewitz' edition of *On War*. If you read the introduction, you'll find that the editors say that you 'can speak the executive's mind because it's your own'. I suspect the great attraction of sketching an intellectual trajectory back to your work is that contemporary strategists can claim foundations of their discipline that transcend the numerical monotony of Excel spreadsheets and the simplicity of 2 x 2 matrices, as well as the resort to phrases like 'out of the box thinking', 'win/win situations', and 'core competencies', all of which conceal the speaker's actual business inexperience (Kornberger, 2013).

ALEXANDER: And the military certainly knows what harm business consultants can do to their organisation. When he arrived at the Department of Defense, Donald Rumsfeld called for a more entrepreneurial approach to war. He favoured what was then in fashion, 'just in time' production. In the marketplace you keep down costs by keeping inventories low. He thought you could do something similar in war by having a light footprint—like invading Iraq with only one-third of the forces you needed to secure victory.

MODERATOR: OK, so much for business strategy. But we're not here to discuss any of this tonight. We're here to look at military strategy.

CLAUSEWITZ: In my book, I claim that strategy is the use of the engagement for the purpose of the war (*On War*, p. 177). It's about political purpose. As one of our own strategic thinkers argues, strategy should serve as a bridge between military power and political purpose. It can and should be the great enabler (Gray, 2015, 21).

MODERATOR: So here's the thing. We've now fought four wars in Lebanon (1983); Somalia (1992–3); Iraq and Afghanistan, and arguably lost every one. Is this because we were out-fought or out-thought? Is this because we lacked a strategy, or because we adopted the wrong one? Let us restrict ourselves just to the last two.

CLAUSEWITZ: Well, I think it all goes back to the very beginning.

Why did you invade Iraq? I think if I were critiquing General Franks' war plan in the run-up to the war, I would probably have asked the same question I did of a young staff officer called Karl von Roeder who wrote to me in 1827 about a staff exercise which predicated a war between Austria and Prussia. I should explain that von Roeder was an intelligent enough young officer, but perhaps not the sharpest tool in the box, and I was very open in my criticism that the staff exercise seemed to ignore politics altogether. Politics, I insisted, and still do, must be the point of departure for any strategic planning.

I found it incredible, for example, that the general staff was planning to mount a staff exercise without first asking what importance the two protagonists were likely to attach to a war? What were their specific strategic objectives: conquest, seizure of territory, or merely a bid to change the balance of power?

In my correspondence with Roeder what I found most puzzling was that nobody on the Prussian staff seemed interested in asking themselves a very simple question: why would Austria want to attack Prussia in 1827? If you look at what was happening at the time, the war didn't break out because there was no reason why it should.

LOWRY: So, General, what reason do you think the Bush administration had for attacking Iraq? Not Weapons of Mass Destruction, surely? It had no new information, though Rumsfeld claimed of course that it saw the existing information through a new prism thanks to 9/11. Iran? Well it was on side on 9/11 and the last thing we wanted was to end up with an Iranian satellite, which we now have. And if we really wanted to kick-start democracy in the Middle East, surely Iraq was something of a backwater? We had to begin where it mattered, in Egypt, or at least Syria. I think you'd have to conclude that the true explanation for the invasion was what our friends in the insurance business call a Moral Hazard. If you're a Formula One racing driver, for example, you tend to drive faster than the rest of us because you know you're better at driving. If you've taken out life insurance for your family, you may be predisposed to take more risks. We invaded Iraq in the end because we could. I suspect that even if Austria had enjoyed a similar military advantage in 1827, its behaviour would have been very different. It was, after all, a different political entity operating in a very different political world.

ALEXANDER: Do you remember in the run-up to the Kosovo War (1999) how many young Kosovars used to sport T-shirts with a variety of the Nike ad: NATO: Just Do It. NATO did, but not because it could. It did it because it felt it had to.

LOWRY: Sure. And because we could invade Iraq we did, and that's why the manner of taking down Saddam was so important: fast, ruthlessly and in defiance of world opinion. What I think we can both agree is that the invasion was mounted in the absence of any real strategic or political ends, and of course it turned out to be a complete disaster.

ALEXANDER: And what was going to happen after Saddam was ousted? Wasn't it the same problem that Napoleon faced when he occupied Moscow? He expected the regime's will to collapse. When it didn't he found himself in trouble. Were the Baathist party or the army going to accept defeat? The army almost certainly would have cut a deal with us. But we disbanded it instead, sending 200,000 men back to their homes with their guns, and leaving those close to Saddam with no alternative but to throw their hat into the ring with the insurgents. Twelve years later they were helping ISIS.

CLAUSEWITZ: Well I think it all goes back to what I said about strategy. And to the importance I attach to theory. You will remember that I insisted that theory educated the mind of a future leader, or rather helped to guide him in self-instruction. But it should never be carried onto the field of battle. In other words, strategic theory is merely an instrument for reflection that prepares a leader for the complexities and subtleties that he encounters in real life. And in order to accomplish such an educational purpose—and this is the point—strategy has to be critical in the application of abstract truth to real events.

And for a strategy to work you really do have to know the situation on the ground, the reality. Your administration told itself a series of stories that it chose to believe despite the evidence: that the invasion would be met with popular support; that your chosen political leaders would be able to hold power; that once the regime fell, the fighting would stop. I wrote that no state goes down without a fight for fear of losing its soul, and the Iraqi state didn't, either (*On War*, 8, 3b). Saddam's generals continued the fight, now with religion being a critical factor.

What theory tells you—or what my theory would have told if you'd taken it to heart—is that reality is never a given. It has to be continually sought out, I'm tempted to say salvaged. Every culture produces a screen partly to facilitate its own practices and partly to allow it to exercise power. It tells itself stories that it finds comforting. Reality is often inimical to those with power for that reason: it forces them, if they're honest, to confront alternative narratives that may reflect the world that is rather than the world one would like.

MODERATOR: And part of that unreality, of course, was the Revolution in Military Affairs?

CLAUSEWITZ: Indeed. One of my principal fans Raymond Aron, wrote some years ago that I didn't do doctrine, only theory, and that theory is 'intended to teach a strategist to understand his task without entertaining any absurd claim to communicate the secret of victory' (Aron, 1983, viii). You remember that your government went into the war saying that the revolution in military affairs guaranteed victory from the start. You scripted the war in advance, and used Iraq as a test case for the RMA. And as part of the script you traded in phrases like 'full-dimensional protection', 'full spectrum dominance' and 'precision engagement'. These were the ideological inflections of your discourse on war at the time.

LOWRY: I remember one US General saying that it offered us the chance to 'abolish Clausewitz'.

CLAUSEWITZ: And it was a bold claim, but not an unexpected one, because I was the man who insisted that in any war chance and friction can never be eliminated, and with them the risk that every conflict entails.

ALEXANDER: Another American general was later to claim that 'dominant battle space awareness' had given way to 'predictive battle space awareness'. One government official went even further. In planning for the future, he remarked, the US military could discard the traditional inductive approach (i.e. learning from history and experience) in favour of a deductive method: it could now posit what the future would look like without reference to the past at all (Buley, 2007, 87). Words reveal a lot, and the terms associated with the RMA—'transformation', 'precision', 'digitalisation' said it all. All tended to downplay the existential value of battle-hardened combat; all played up a degree of control in an era in which we boasted that we enjoyed 'full spectrum dominance'. We have subsequently found that the RMA is merely the latest in a long wish-list of techno-scientific panaceas that have been sold as benefits without costs—like the 'peaceful atom', the space programme and modern eugenics.

CLAUSEWITZ: I'd say you actually failed in Iraq from the very beginning, on the theoretical plane. You chose to airbrush out of your plan of campaign anything that was likely to get in the way of a positive outcome. You dismissed friction, which I claimed is the only conception that in a general way corresponds to that which distinguishes real war from war on paper. When you encountered unexpected opposition on the way to Baghdad from local fighters, you were strong enough to brush them aside, but they later reformed and became an important part of the insurgency.

You may recall that I identified the particular preconditions under which prediction in war would be possible when you thought you'd satisfied all three conditions: 1) when a war is a completely isolated act and is in no way connected with the previous history of the enemy state; 2) when the outcome is limited to a single decision; and 3) when it contains within itself a solution which is perfect and complete, free from any reaction upon it. In reality, none of these conditions can ever be met in the real world.

ALEXANDER: Surely strategy is all about consequences, and I think we can say with some assurance that we never did consequence management in the case of Iraq.

CLAUSEWITZ: The problem's not only one of political misjudgement, though the fallibility of human understanding and the limits to human knowledge will always cast a permanent shadow over what you like to call 'decision dominance', the speed with which on the basis of knowledge, the military can arrive at a decision. The problem is more profound. It inheres in complexity. It's always impossible to anticipate and therefore insure against all the effects of going to war, which is why I said that you should never take a first step without considering the last. You should always be preoccupied with the consequences of your own actions, the side-effects if you like. Unpredictability is a product of every conflict and you have to live with it.

ALEXANDER: I'm afraid we took Shock and Awe at face value, namely that we had taken war into the twenty-first century with a vengeance. And so we had, but only in relation to the kill chain. In 1991 Desert Storm started with a long drawn out bombing campaign and then a ground assault. In 2003 we were able to provide bombers with the co-ordinates for their bombs. In 1991 it had taken days of paper-pushing to assign a plane a target. During Operation Iraqi Freedom it took under ten minutes. But for all that, we found that we'd only changed the dynamics of a network-enabled process—killing.

The most important network was the social world that linked clans and tribes. We put too little emphasis in the early days of the campaign on securing key urban areas and government buildings, which created security gaps that led to firefights, ambushes and quite soon extensive looting. Another telling failure emerged from the *Army Lessons Learned Reports* after December 2003. It was found that the greatest intelligence assets were soldiers on foot patrol who were able to establish a 'ground truth' which often conflicted with the analysis of the commanders behind the line. But the number of patrols was limited by the number of vehicles available. Our troops were trained to deal with symmetrical war; they were not trained to deal with looting, or to distinguish hostile and non-violent civilians from insurgents. They were not trained to deal with the consequences of victory (Cordesman, 2003, 499).

LOWRY: One of the main reasons, of course, that we could mount so few foot patrols, was because we'd gone in with an insufficiently large force in the belief that we would be greeted as liberators. Any prospect that this would be true was vitiated by our failure to provide basic services, such as water and electricity. And the crime surge which exacerbated popular insecurity owed much to the failure of our post-conflict planning. It didn't take long for looters, ex-convicts and nihilistic jobless youths to realise that banding together would give them a collective power to rob, mug and otherwise get a Darwinian foothold in the local economy. And as the insurgency gathered pace, political actors like al-Qaeda exploited the crime wave to fund its own activities. Although the insurgents often ordered the kidnappings, they outsourced them to criminal gangs.

MODERATOR: But didn't we get lucky in 2007 when we decided to boost our force in Iraq in what's called the Surge? Didn't it work, at least for a time? Didn't we arrive at a strategic objective: preventing civil war within a new strategic context as the Sunni tribes identified with us against a common enemy, al-Qaeda?

ALEXANDER: I agree the Surge worked for a time. Security improved and connections were built up with local tribes and al-Qaeda was put on the back foot, but it was also strategically inconclusive. None of the political questions that powered the insurgency were resolved: who to share the country's oil revenues with, and how; what would be the relationship between the three main groups (Shi'a, Sunni and the Kurds); and whether Iraq would emerge as a weak confederation or a strong state. And then we made the mistake of putting the insurgents in an internment camp called Camp Bucca, which we named after a New York firefighter who lost his life on 9/11. Over 20,000 Iraqi insurgents, mostly Sunni, were incarcerated until its final closure in 2011. What did the detainees do in their spare time? They spent endless hours studying the Koran and discussing military strategy. Camp Bucca was in effect a terrorist training school. Unwittingly we created conditions in which the seeds of Islamic State were sown: the most famous inmate being the self-proclaimed Caliph Abu-Bakr al-Baghdadi. And here's something else. Baghdadi's second-in-command was a member of Saddam Hussein's feared military intelligence, and his second deputy was a Major-General in Saddam's army. What happened was that the Baathist party members rediscovered their faith.

LOWRY: The ultimate irony is that we were so determined to avoid repeating previous mistakes that we went on to make mistakes no-one had ever made before.

MODERATOR: Sure thing, Bob. But let me press you on another point, General Clausewitz. There's an argument that it's difficult to set strategic goals in any case because you're always going to be surprised by events. Paul Wolfowitz, one of the principal architects of the invasion, claimed that 'the whole of the last century is littered with failures of prediction.' We didn't predict what happened on 9/11; we didn't predict the war would continue in Afghanistan after the fall of the Taliban; we didn't predict that once the conventional phase of operations was over in Iraq the war would morph into a counter-insurgency campaign which we came very close to losing. The Iraq War made President Bush the most disastrous President of modern times. It destroyed Donald Rumsfeld's career as well as his reputation.

But here's the thing, General. All wars have unintended consequences, don't they? It really is almost impossible to do what you advise: never plan the first move without thinking about the last. In fact, two of your critics point out that many of the wars that we have fought have not ended neatly when hostilities have ceased and treaties signed. We have been forced to defend the post-war settlement for years to come. Their contention is that war cannot be what you said it should be—the continuation of politics by other means—in other words a rational and legitimate means of furthering national interests. On the contrary, they suggest most wars produce an entirely new policy. Let me read out a quote from their book: 'Hannah Arendt observed that "politics is the realm of unintended consequences." She was drawing attention to the distinction between the predictable world of mechanics and computers and the world of politicians who cannot accurately predict the consequences of their actions. If this is true of politics, it is even more true of war, which is why the notion that war is merely policy by other means is nonsense." (Hagan/Bickerton, 2007).

Care to comment?

CLAUSEWITZ: I don't think the authors understand my book any more than do most of my other critics. I doubt whether many people have much grasp of the complexities and nuances of the message I was trying to get across. Even your own military has embraced an a-strategic culture (for years it defined strategy as the art of bringing the enemy to the battlefield). Nonsense—it's the art of transforming a tactical success into a conclusive strategic and therefore political outcome.

And I want to make another point. Even the way you choose to wage war is disturbingly apolitical. You are fixated on speed because of domestic politics: wars need to be short for them to be politically acceptable. Of course that, too, is a reflection that my claim that war is a part of the province of social life. But if that's the only way you can fight wars, perhaps you should think twice about waging them.

LOWRY: Speed kills, General Franks tells us in his memoirs.

CLAUSEWITZ: A very good illustration of my point. In my book I argued that it is impossible to generalise without engaging in a soulless analysis.

The 'evil' of generalisation is another example of the discrepancy between what you're taught in the classroom and what you know to be real once you are on the ground. It becomes what I called an inadmissible one-sided formal code of law. It becomes an axiom that may be true in one situation, but quite untrue in another.

LOWRY: It's a feature of our times, General, our obsession with exit strategies and cut-off points and our desire always to draw a line under events and move on. There's a striking passage in Milan Kundera's novel *Slowness* (1995) in which one of the characters reflects upon the sheer speed of news broadcasts, as he mulls over how fragments give way to new fragments in no particular order and which do not lend themselves as a result to any over-arching narrative. It becomes impossible to weave these snippets of news into the larger tapestry we call history, because everyone is waiting for the next news flash. Instead history is narrated in the same way that at a concert the orchestra plays all of Beethoven's 138 works consecutively, but only the first eight bars of each. In another ten years, reflects Kundera, they'll only play the first note of each piece—138 notes altogether. And in twenty years the whole of Beethoven's music will be summed up in a single very long buzzing tone like the endless sound he heard the first day of his deafness (Eriksen, 2001, 49). The story should resonate with you as Beethoven was a contemporary of yours.

ALEXANDER: 'Speed kills' General Franks tells us but it didn't help us win the war. We sped to failure, not success, precisely because we thought of speed as a theoretical axiom that always had to be applied. Looking back at the insurgency, even George Bush lamented that we had become the victims of our 'catastrophic success'. Or as our former Chairman of the Joint Chiefs asserted, our victory in Iraq was simply too 'elegant'. What both men meant is that we won too quickly. It may seem counter-intuitive to this audience, but we know from history that a society is more likely to accept defeat, and a country only prevails in war when it does so (as you remind us, General Clausewitz), when the defeated society is reconciled to defeat, and usually then only after a long struggle like Germany and Japan in 1945. Moreover, if a society puts up a good fight at least, there's really no shame in surrender. But when it collapses in three weeks, demoralisation may set in and in no time become both toxic and morally corrosive. We used to call some of the insurgents POIs—Pissed Off Iraqis. They were young men who simply wanted to regain their honour

LOWRY: Speed unfortunately takes no account of complexity, which is why the direction in which we're taking war is so counter-productive. Every obstacle, like the Fedayeen fighters who appeared unexpectedly as we advanced towards Baghdad, was seen as a temporary obstacle to be bypassed or pushed aside. But that's the point. Obstacles don't always disappear—they're merely side-lined for the moment. They reappear at unexpected and inconvenient moments later on. They're often the warning signs not to transgress certain limits.

MODERATOR: Might we explore this a little further? Speed takes no account of complexity. In your book, General Clausewitz, you write that the great general should reduce the complex to the simple. Many writers today would agree with this approach. Herbert

Simon, one of the founders of complexity theory insists the purpose of all theory is to understand the meaningful simplicity in the midst of complexity (Buchanan, 2002, 214). Computer games suggest that behaviour may be extraordinarily complex, yet it also generates rules. The behaviour of stock markets and political systems may be relatively easy to understand thanks to agent-based modelling.

CLAUSEWITZ: It's difficult to define what simplicity and complexity actually are, of course. A battle plan, for example, can be grasped very quickly, but what it involves is a very complex set of moving parts. Ask why a battle plan goes wrong, and you're in difficult territory. In the end your obsession with speed simply flies in the face of friction. Everything looks simple until one has to carry it out. And the simplest thing then becomes very difficult. Friction can't be conjured away by technology or politics. It is the only concept that encapsulates the factors that distinguish real war from the war you'd like to fight, the war on paper (*On War*, 7, 1).

ALEXANDER: There's a famous passage in your book, General, in which you describe how a traveller decides to cover two more stages before nightfall. Only four or five hours more on a paved highway, with relays of horses, it should be an easy trip. But at the next station he finds there are no fresh horses, only very poor ones. And as he progresses, the country grows hilly and the roads become bad, and then night falls. You say it's much the same in war. Countless minor incidents—the kind you can never really foresee—combine to lower the general level of performance so that one always falls short of one's intended goal. In other words, unintended consequences are a fact of life and one must craft a strategy accordingly.

And that's precisely what's so difficult. Armies like ours are exploitative; they are governed by doctrines and standard operational procedures. Insurgents are explorative systems that mutate quickly by adapting to their environment. It's only by readapting in adverse circumstances that they survive at all. Unlike armies they don't have mass or inertia. They travel quickly because they carry less baggage. They can dematerialise and rematerialize at will.

MODERATOR: Well isn't one way to deal with this to get better intelligence on our adversaries?

ALEXANDER: Might I suggest that one of the problems we face is that we rely so much on faulty intelligence. One of your greatest twentieth century critics, General Clausewitz, surprisingly agreed with you when it came to your scepticism about the use of intelligence. Looking back over the last 150 years in his book *Intelligence in War*, he wrote that willpower always accounted for more than foreknowledge. Ultimately it's force not forethought that counts (Keegan, 2004, 334).

CLAUSEWITZ: Well this is certainly true of tactical intelligence in battle. I don't think it's always true of operational intelligence (the management of a campaign), and it's not usually true of strategic intelligence, which often influences the decision to go to war or not.

ALEXANDER: Perhaps we have too much information, that's the problem, and much of what we have is ambiguous and contradictory. And here's another thing. It's the 'unknown unknowns' that frighten us the most. The things we don't give any attention to because they're unknowable, until that is they suddenly occur. You argue that intelligence is of limited value. You claim, if I remember rightly, that a greater part of the information obtained is contradictory, a still greater part usually false, and by far the greatest part of doubtful character. You were talking about the knowledge that could be gained about probabilities of enemy intentions.

CLAUSEWITZ: Information is, of course, the fundamental element in war: our knowledge of the enemy and the country in which we're operating, to take two examples. War, I explain, is the 'province of uncertainty'. Part of the uncertainty comes from faulty intelligence. I was identifying an interesting paradox: the more information we have, the more our uncertainty seems to increase. Every piece of information brings a new detail into focus, yet the potential connections between these pieces of information explode with each new detail. Formulaically, as information increases linearly, potential relations between pieces of data explode exponentially.

LOWRY: Information processing, of course, continues to improve, or so we're told. But I think we should keep our sense of proportion. If you hang around Silicon Valley or watch enough Ted Talks, you'll probably encounter 'learnings' that go down well in Palo Alto— you know the kind of thing: we've accumulated more information in the past two years than we have since the dawn of civilisation. But just hold that thought for the moment. An IMF economist in 2001 analysed the accuracy of economic forecasts in the 1990s and found they had all failed to predict recession. When he looked at the forecasts in 2001–2014 he found that despite an exponential increase in data, they were no better than they had been in the previous decade (*The Times*, 4 August, 2015). In real life, uncertainty arises not from gaps in knowledge; it arises very largely from lack of comprehension. So don't try for 100 per cent information, but accept uncertainty. In any armed conflict success depends, as you say in your book, on an ability to tolerate uncertainty, cope with it and even exploit it (Bousquet, 2011, 242).

MODERATOR: So we come back to the fact that we went into Iraq thinking we knew more than we did, and when things began to go pear-shaped we found we couldn't process the new information quickly enough. Which brings us to one of your most famous concepts, General: the fog of war. You can't always see over the top of the hill. The fog of war, you said, tends to make things seem grotesque and larger than they really are.

ALEXANDER: General, the thought that you can abolish the fog of war is one that we in the US military find very seductive. Let me tell you a story that Malcolm Gladwell relates about a war game which involved one of my fellow Marines, Paul van Riper. In the spring of 2000 the General was approached by a group of Pentagon officials to take part in a war game that involved forty-two separate computer models and simulated actions and lasted 2.5 weeks. It was intended to show that in the twenty-first century the battlefield had become increasingly transparent thanks to satellites and super-computers.

Van Riper was tasked with playing the role of the enemy commander. The US side knocked out his microwave towers and cut his fibre optic lines, hoping he would be forced to use satellite communications and cell phones which they could hack into. Instead, he did the unexpected. He communicated with members of his team using couriers on motorcycles and messages hidden inside prayer books. He created the conditions for successful spontaneity by allowing his juniors to be innovative. He didn't allow long meetings. He thus made a nonsense of the attempt by the rival team to create perfect knowledge by creating an Operational Net Assessment which broke the enemy into a series of sub-sets: economic, social, political and military, a tool that was supposed to banish the fog of war.

CLAUSEWITZ: So Van Riper won the game?

ALEXANDER: Get with the programme, General. No, the organisers merely changed the game. They re-ran it, this time fully scripted. They allowed no opportunities for the complexities of the real world to intrude, and the fog of war was miraculously lifted.

As Gladwell writes, the episode proved to be a battle between two opposing military philosophies (Gladwell, 2005, 108) and van Riper represented the school of thought that was—you might say—thoroughly Clausewitzian.

MODERATOR: Can I move to one last point. It involves another of the concepts for which you are truly famous. Could it be said that we made the grave mistake in Iraq of never identifying the correct centre of gravity? We disbanded the army, even though it was the only stabilising force that could have helped us to retain control of the country. And the insurgency, remember, was conducted by many former members of the Army. We even allowed soldiers to return home with their arms and later sell them in what became the largest small arms market in history.

CLAUSEWITZ: The centre of gravity unfortunately has been interpreted in purely physical terms: such as an opponent's army. Alexander's centre of gravity, I argued, was indeed his army. Sometimes, however, it is the enemy's capital city; Vienna was for Napoleon in the 1809 war, but Moscow wasn't in the 1812. The Russians burned down their own capital. But the concept more widely considered can include unity of interests and public opinion. I really wanted to concentrate on the enemy's motivation. I wrote that it's not by conquering provinces with superior numbers, or defeating an army in line that matters, but seeking out the 'heart of the hostile power'. Values, beliefs and interests are the key (*On War*, 8, 4). The Iraqi army should have been seen not in material terms, but in terms of a moral order: the sum of its means and strength of its will. It is the enemy's strength of will that is often difficult to determine, and can only be estimated to a certain extent by the strength of its motives for engaging in war (*On War*, 1, 1).

Ultimately, it is important to identify not the concentrated force—an army in being which in this case had been defeated in the field—but the thing that causes it to concentrate and give it purpose and direction. I was critical of Napoleon, for example, in his 1814 campaign for engaging with the Prussian and Austrian armies at different times. Instead of concentrating his forces against the principal enemy, the Prussian army led by Blucher, he engaged in secondary battles against the Austrians. Of the two, the Prussian force was the more important because although numerically weaker, it had greater spirit and was much more committed to securing Napoleon's unconditional defeat. If it had been forced into retreat, the Austrians would have joined them soon enough (*On War*, 2, 5).

ALEXANDER: In his memoirs, Franks reveals that Rumsfeld had never heard of the centre of gravity. He thought that once Baghdad fell, so would the regime. But Franks himself was all at sea—in the same memoirs he talks of nine slices representing Iraqi centres of gravity which constituted a 'working matrix' of targets. They ranged from the leadership to internal security. This was a relentlessly operational approach. Franks thought it was the 'grand strategy of the campaign' but there was nothing strategic about it. He failed to identify one centre of gravity: instead he identified nine (Ricks, 2012, 128).

LOWRY: Remember the great line from *Alice through the Looking Glass*? When you don't know where you're going, all roads lead there. There are many different centres of gravity. In the 1960s the *Mini Manual of*

Urban Warfare identified the strategic centre of gravity as the link between state and society: provoke the state into eroding its legitimacy in the eyes of society by over-reacting and suspending civil liberties, and you would in effect get it to attack itself. In the case of Iraq, the centre of gravity was an army that had interests that it wished to preserve. It was, of course, unfortunate that it did not decide in 1991 to mount a coup against Saddam when he was at his weakest, after the end of the First Gulf War.

ALEXANDER: Our discussion of the centre of gravity illustrates what was wrong about the whole operation from the very start. It was a strategic blunder of epic proportions—that we can all agree on—and our failure was all the more dismaying for coming after sixteen months of planning and preparation. We made the mistake of focusing exclusively on a plan of attack rather than the difficult but more crucial idea of consolidating victory. Representative Ike Skelton wrote a letter to the President in September 2002, he quoted you, General Clausewitz: he reminded the White House that the first requirement of war is 'not to take the first step without considering the last' (Ricks, 2006, 59). He had no doubt at all that we would defeat Saddam's forces with comparative ease, but like the proverbial dog chasing the car down the road, we really had to consider what to do after catching it.

MODERATOR: Can we move on to Afghanistan, as time is pressing. This was the longest war in our history and its outcome is still unclear. Any thoughts, gentlemen?

CLAUSEWITZ: Let me ask a question. How did it happen that having crushed al-Qaeda and forced Taliban from power, you got involved in state-building, nation-building and democracy promotion?

LOWRY: The basic goal of our mission became what science fiction writers call terra-forming. We wanted to

refashion Afghanistan as a modern, secular, democratic society. The basic assumption behind that goal
was that the Afghan people would want what we
wanted for them, or that they would want what we
wanted them to want.

CLAUSEWITZ: And that, if I may say, was a fundamental error of
judgement. You simply didn't understand the culture
of the society you were dealing with.

ALEXANDER: Not that we didn't try, General. A few years into the
campaign we engaged a number of anthropologists in
a controversial project called the Human Terrain
System which we rolled out in 2007. It was the largest
single investment ever made by the Department of
Defense in applied social science. It was a $150m a
year programme that was quietly terminated in 2014
in the wake of mounting criticism both from within
the military and the academic profession.

MODERATOR: Could you say a little bit more about your own
approach to culture, General?

CLAUSEWITZ: Well, as you may know, the word doesn't appear in my
book. In my day it was more common to speak of a
people's 'manners and customs'. What was customary
was considered constitutive of a particular way of life
(Shweder, 2000, 163). I think it's always best with any
concept, but especially one as amorphous as culture,
to narrow it down so that it includes less and reveals
more. Culture in that sense can be seen as contextu-
alisation—war has a social, economic, historical, even
geographical context.

My earliest contribution to the debate was an essay I
wrote after being taken prisoner after the Battle of
Auerstadt. During my months in captivity I tried to
nail down the factors that accounted for the French
success on the battlefield. Was there something in the
German national character, I asked, that might account

for our catastrophic defeat? The answer to my own question contained—I'm afraid to say—some rather crude thoughts about the connection between politics and culture. Some of my observations were pretty banal, I'm the first to admit. But it's an interesting object lesson in an attempt to nail down a culture (and in this case not always getting it right). For example, I concluded that the French were superficial; they grasped a point quickly but rarely got to the bottom of it.

LOWRY: Aldous Huxley famously observed that you Germans dived deeper to the bottom of the river than anyone else and invariably came up muddier as a result. You concluded that the French had too little originality of mind. Huxley thought you Germans had too much.

CLAUSEWITZ: Too true, perhaps. But then if you read my essay you'll see that I claimed the French were more tractable politically, more subservient to the State, less individualistic than we Germans. And the French Revolution had confirmed that they were at heart centrists. The result of my enquiry led me to conclude that they were more easily pressed into uniform, and were frankly better at war because of it (Pait, 1992, 250—62).

But all of this was germane to the reason I wrote my book. When and why should a society go to war against another? What I thought inexcusable was that we'd gone to war against the French twice, in 1792 and 1806, without any understanding of the enemy we faced. Would we have invaded France in 1792, I asked, if we had known that if we failed to win it would have emboldened the Revolutionary Government to overthrow the whole European balance of power? We should have remembered that while the French Assembly two years earlier had concluded with a declaration of its commitment to peace, it had also warned that if France had to fight it would defend itself with 'newly righteous fury' (Bell, 2007). It wasn't the French Revolution that reshaped the European order, but the French Revolutionary Wars. Would we have gone to war against France in 1806 if we'd known 'that the first shot would have set off a mine that would blow her to the skies' (Porter, 2009, 190)? And would you for that matter have invaded Iraq if you'd known that it would blow up the Middle East and spark off what is likely to be decades of conflict in the region? Would you have attempted to fundamentally change the social and political order in Afghanistan if you'd known that in doing so you would create an even greater problem for yourself?

LOWRY: Yes indeed. We intervened where the poet Horace advised epic poets to begin their tale—*in media res*—in the middle of the story. Only in this case, of course, it wasn't our story, but someone else's. You will recall that Homer plunges his readers into the ninth year of the Trojan War, not the first. But he knew that his readers would know the story from childhood; we didn't in Afghanistan. We imagined that ideas like human rights and democracy and freedom had a power to transform the lives of everyone. But in the end we left, choosing to let the Afghan army to fight it out on its own, not because our goals had been achieved, but because we had given up on them.

The whole episode reminds me, by the way, of a story by Bruce Sterling called *Mozart in Mirror Shades* (1985) in which some time in the future time travel helps companies to extract mineral resources from a pre-industrial past. The author neatly gets around the time paradox—what happens if you meet your grandfather and accidentally kill him so that you can't be born—by positing that as soon as the present makes contact with a specific moment in the past, that strand of time forks off from recorded history and leads towards an alternative future. Similar thinking, I fear, belied our nation-building efforts. We arrived from the future into a pre-modern present, hoping it would fork off towards an alternative future that would not unfold but for our intervention.

ALEXANDER: But you know the real problem our generals confronted was that there was no real political direction. You can be tactically brilliant and operationally successful, but it's the politicians who set the political objectives which the tactics are intended to serve. We executed missions, but not campaigns, for that reason, writes General McChrystal in his memoirs (McChrystal, 2013, 181). Neither Bush nor Obama ever really spelled out what their political goals were. At one time I counted eight or more, from nation-building, state-building, democracy promotion, sending girls to school, opium eradication and infrastructure building—everything but actually winning the war. And as for cultural knowledge—how do you eliminate the opium on which two-thirds of the population has come to depend for their livelihoods? Sure, most Afghan fathers wanted their daughters to go to school, but it wasn't priority number one; the safety and security of their families was. The importance of the local actually matters, particularly when the locals know you're not going to be there forever. I think our fundamental failure was to appreciate that ordinary people, oddly enough, have ordinary concerns (Ledwidge, 2011, 2007).

MODERATOR: So gentlemen, could anything have been achieved in Afghanistan where the level of cultural sensitivity was so low?

LOWRY: In Afghanistan the very notion of 'best solution' was fundamentally misconceived. We needed to come up with a different way of thinking. We needed to see

Afghanistan for what it was—a society that had survived relatively intact because of its own internal ability to adapt to outside invaders. Afghanistan wasn't broken before we arrived.

ALEXANDER: We were on a hiding to nothing from the very beginning. Once NATO got involved there were a number of stakeholders each with their own frames of reference. There was no single right solution. The way in which you frame the question will influence the solution you come up with. And every so-called solution or attempt to implement it changed the problem. We all became part of the problem once we intervened. In the end we ran out of patience and left.

LOWRY: The Roman historian Dio Cassius offers some useful advice that we would be well advised to heed in future. We remember the wars between the Greeks and the Persians as a great struggle for freedom largely because Herodotus wrote about it this way. And we remember the total defeat of the Persian forces and their expulsion from Greece. Dio Cassius, however, tells us that the Persians themselves constructed a very different narrative. They announced to the world that they had indeed invaded Greece, burned down Athens and taken thousands of prisoners who were subsequently sold into slavery. In other words they had taught the Greeks no end of a lesson. 'Mission Accomplished'.

MODERATOR: What do you think of that, General?

CLAUSEWITZ: I'm pretty amazed. You allow tactics to drive your strategic ambition. But perhaps such an approach reflects changing political realities, and social needs. Perhaps, it is a feature of the changing character of war.

MODERATOR: On that note, General, I think we should end. By the way, I understand that you've been asked by a New York publishing house to write a sequel to *On War*?

REBOOTING CLAUSEWITZ

CLAUSEWITZ: I told them to think again. I've said everything I have to say.

LOWRY: But you should re-think the matter, Sir. It would at least give your first book the flavour of a movie franchise.

120

5

ON MILITARY HISTORY

CLAUSEWITZ AT THE MILITARY HISTORY CIRCLE, LONDON

I meet the general at the entrance to the Army and Navy Club (the In and Out as its members call it, founded in 1837). He is in town as a guest of the Royal College of Defence Studies (another venerable institution) where he is delivering a lecture on the future of war. He is a little stiff, though we get over that with a drink at the bar—he seems rather abstemious in his habits though, and not a little reserved, even unbending. But we have a few members like that—academics can be very stand-offish.

It is a little embarrassing to have to tell him that our Military History Circle, which dates back to the 1930s, was founded by Basil Liddel Hart. There is a brief hiatus in the conversation; they obviously had issues. Anyway steady the buffs as we say—or used to back in Basil's day. Oh, I should tell you something about myself, though there is not that much to tell. Our Circle is made up largely of military historians, of course, but the sherpas—people like me—tend to be ex-officers (retired). I am the secretary and have the job of meeting our speakers, setting them at ease and explaining our procedures. Clausewitz seems to be impressed by the club anyway with its portraits of the great and good looking down on the members.

We are joined at the bar by Professor Lindeman who is chairing the meeting. He is an Oxford man with a good range in anecdotes. The one

the general warms to most was the story of a don from All Souls—
that's the college without students—who back in the 1890s was often
approached by visitors who had been prompted to ask the same question: 'We understand, sir, that when you were a very young lad in
Torbay you were once rowed out to see the Emperor Napoleon pacing
up and down the deck of the *HMS Bellerophon* which was taking him
into exile on St Helena. 'Quite true, young man', was the invariable
reply, 'though he wasn't an emperor then, just a general.' 'Might we
ask,' the visitors would usually persist, 'what impression he made upon
you?'. 'Oh, you could tell at a glance that he wasn't a "university man."'

That seems to amuse our guest, who of course wasn't a university
man either. A whiskey or two later, we toddle off to dinner in a private
room. The members are all there—almost a full house, and we sit
down to dine. The format is simple enough—two courses, then the
speaker says a few words of introduction before the discussion begins.
Pretty relaxed, don't you think? Though some of our Profs are pretty
sharp, especially with each other. But this evening we have agreed that
it will be a free-for-all—we all know the General's work after all, and
we are here to discuss one particular aspect for which he is famous—
the importance he attached to military history.

Clausewitz begins the proceedings by thanking us for the invitation.
'I had hoped to get the London embassy, as you probably know, but
such was not my destiny. I was told that I was considered too radical
even by the English, who opposed my appointment. And I know I have
few friends in your navy; my critics still like to remind me that I was
silent on the use of naval power. I must plead *mea culpa*—Thucydides
opened his *History* with a discussion of naval power, so you may consider he has a distinct advantage over me at least in this regard.'

Lindeman ripostes: 'We won't hold it against you, General. Welcome
to our little circle anyway. I hope we will have a good discussion this
evening. I tell my students that in some ways you are more of a military
historian than a social scientist. Your last work after all, was an analysis
of the 1799 campaign—you even put off working on your book. At
900 pages it is almost as long as *On War*!'

'So let me kick off by asking you what you consider to be the place of
military history in your general theory of war. There are, I would say,
three types of historical enquiry. The first relates to the nature of history

itself: how do we best "read" the past; what is the scope of human agency and of social forces: do great men and women drive events; is it possible for any historian to grasp History's "secret harmonies" (if they are there to be found)? How we get to our point of departure is always the most interesting part of the journey, don't you think?'

'The second approach involves the interpretation of evidence in the form of written texts and primary sources and eyewitness accounts, data-crunching if you will, and here there are many parallels with the endeavours of scientists. Finally, historians also investigate existential experiences; rituals and conventions and codes of honour and the mentalities of particular societies. After science, historical knowledge for us in the West is probably the most important form of knowledge, although there are many other forms such as literature and the arts. A great novelist, for example, may be able to illuminate aspects of reality we would not otherwise have seen unless he had shown them to us. So, where, General, do you fit into this picture? I think, if I may presume to anticipate your answer, that your own approach is the second. But if so where does the study of history fit into your general theory of war?'

'Well', replies Clausewitz, slightly peeved (I imagine) by the length of the so-called introduction (Lindeman does like the sound of his own voice). 'I would agree with your proposition. As to your question, I first learnt the importance of history from my mentor, Scharnhorst, who put history at the centre of military education. His approach was entirely utilitarian in inspiration. You know the quote: "History is philosophy teaching by examples"? It is often attributed to Thucydides.'

'Actually, General, he may have got it from his own teacher, Anaxagoras', pipes up Professor Jones (a bit of a pedant, I always think; likes to impress us with 'devil in the detail' stuff). 'Quite so,' says Clausewitz. 'Many years later I wrote that you should never entertain an idea unless you can back it up with an historical example. Secondly, every theory needs to be grounded in experience (often historical). Thirdly, an historical example often illustrates the possibility that a theoretical argument may be true. And fourthly, in some cases it may even act as "proof" of a theoretical proposition.' (*On War*, 2, 6)

'What I think makes your study of history especially important', continues Lindeman, 'is that you interpreted every period according to its own measure; you refused to judge the past, in other words, purely by the standards of your own day (Paret, 1992, 4). This often put you at odds with contemporary historians. But it also put you in synch with the more rigorous scientific study that we identify with the professional historians of the twentieth century like your fellow countryman Ranke'.

'Not to mention the fact,' adds Professor Sullivan (she is the great expert on eighteenth century warfare), 'that you put great emphasis on the study of comparative history. We take this for granted but in your day that was quite innovatory. Whether you were discussing the Wars of the Spanish and Austrian Succession, or offering a strategic critique of Napoleon's 1814 campaign, you were always asking the most salient question: how did war differ from your own day and why? Why did Louis XIV fail to lead his armies into battle as his predecessors had done, and what did this say about French society in 1700? These are all examples of what Lukacs calls historical thinking—our knowledge of the present is actually dependent on our knowledge of the past (and the contrast between the two). He goes on to add that history is not a social science so much as a form of thought—hence the saying that we live forward, but only think backward.' (Lukacs, 2005, 7).

'Well', Clausewitz responds, 'my main aim in writing my book was to provide a theoretical framework that would help the reader to understand why the wars of the past were different from those of my day'.

'Might I observe,' Lindeman interjects, 'that you found yourself struggling with the fundamental question confronting every historian. When interpreting a historical phenomenon such as war, how do we combine the individuality given by our sources with the general abstract knowledge that makes it possible to interpret the individual sources in the first place? How do we arrive at an empirically secure statement about the larger processes of history? Usually professional historians prefer to leave the larger questions to social scientists. So, I would conclude that your tendency to generalise is more consistent with our understanding of the use of history by social scientists rather than its use by historians'.

Professor Sullivan chips in at this point. 'I wonder if we might move on to specifics. I want to make a more general point about causation. There were quite a few thinkers in your day—'military philosophers' they were called—who had a lot to say about the principles of war. But they did not theorise very successfully. You were the first important theorist. And what confirmed you in this role was your ambition (we read from a note you penned in 1827) "to engender a revolution in the theory of war." (Heuser, 2002, 5) What was truly "revolutionary" was your dual strategy of embracing Newton's scientific method and at the same time rejecting Newtonian reductionism. That is very important for historians—our currency, after all, is causation.'

Clausewitz seems to warm to this question. 'Newton was important not only for laws which brought order to chaos—most famously the law of gravitation—but also for being able to demonstrate them through experiment. This was the importance of his book *Optics* (1704) which drew conclusions on the nature of light thanks entirely to the experimental method. Remember that the word experiment was a fairly recent invention in his day. *Experimentia* (experience) and *experimentum* (experiment) had been more or less synonymous until then. This is not to deny that experiments had been conducted for a long time, but they had been used to fill gaps in a fundamentally deductive system of knowledge. After Newton they involved the replication of results. Newton went on to propound a number of classic Laws such as "for every action there is an equal and opposite reaction." Physical bodies are attracted to each other directly in proportion to their mass or indirectly in proportion to their distance from each other. A planet (to invoke the famous origin of the law of gravitation) could be said to be merely an overgrown apple (Caputo, 2013, 127). Remember though, I always insisted that on no account should theory raise itself to the level of a law. And the reason why is pretty simple. Agreed, war has certain universal features but you can't attach fixed values to those universals. It is impossible to attach a value to each of the three elements: primordial violence/enmity; chance/probability and policy/reason. The context is everything: and in turn it is the relationship between the three that will determine the character of the war in question (Aron, 1983, 85).'

'Where I broke with the Newtonian thinking of the day was its reductionism—the belief that everything could be explained in material terms. It reached an absurd endgame at the end of the eighteenth century in the work of Pierre Simon Laplace, the great French mathematician who postulated on the basis of Newtonian mechanics that life, the universe and everything in it, could be described by a world equation of the vector form: $dX/dt=F(X)$. This formula was the basis, he thought, for the laws of causality.'

Professor Manchester (Cambridge) butts in: 'When Napoleon asked him where God was in such a system, Laplace famously replied that he had no need "for that particular hypothesis." Laplace rejected God out of hand but he also embraced the rigid idea that $A+B=C$ on all occasions and in all situations. To his mind the world was a predictable place, and human behaviour subject to similar laws which remained only to be identified in due course. What you, Sir, were in effect rejecting was the Newtonian understanding of causation. What you didn't know at the time of course was that Newtonian science would be challenged by scientists themselves before the end of the nineteenth century. With the advent of quantum science the idea of "laws" took a knock. At the subatomic level—the world turns out to be far from Newtonian. And some systems, like the weather, are inherently unpredictable because of their acute sensitivity to initial conditions.'

'Our understanding of the world is necessarily incomplete and highly contingent. We can never know all the determining factors or elements of the present. Take the famous Heisenberg Principle, which tells us that an object changes in the act of observation. Actually, the Uncertainty Principle, as we know it in the English-speaking world, is a mistranslation (Krause, 2015, 253)'. I can't help noting he loses most of his audience at this point—he is the Circle bore and never misses an opportunity to score a point whenever he finds an opening. 'The actual word he used was *unschärferelation*, which translates (as you will know, General), into an "un-sharpness relationship". But as there is no such word in English and all possibilities such as "vague" or "ambiguous" were found wanting, the translation ended up as "Uncertainty Principle." What Heisenberg meant, in fact, was "as yet undetermined," not undeterminable. But the overall proposition still holds: the act of studying an event can change it. Anthropologists know that when they study a tribe their behaviour may change once they know they are being observed. This was the famous mistake of Margaret Mead in trying to observe the sex lives of the Samoans. The theorist of war is at one and the same time observer and actor, part and parcel of the social world she seeks to explore.'

Manchester continues to drone on regardless of the glazed eyes in the room. 'Then there is Heisenberg's second proposition: what we observe is not nature itself but nature exposed to our method of questioning. A theory in part constructs a reality. Reality exists independent of the observer of course but our perceptions of reality are influenced by the theories framing our examination of it. That is why Liddell Hart was so critical of you, by the way, General. He was convinced that had the generals not read your book and tried to realise your penchant for the decisive battle they would not have persevered with the horrendously costly offensives of 1916–17.'

'And then there is the breakdown of the mechanical nature of causality. Even in physics, causation—the idea that A equals B—is fundamentally un-demonstrable. Causes tend to be complex. In *War and Peace* Tolstoy challenged basic Newtonian ideas of causation. Why does an apple fall from a particular tree? Certainly, the law of gravity is one explanation, but gravity only explains why it fell to earth. The correct answer may be more prosaic; the stem withered; or the apple was dried out by the sun; or wind shook the branches. The French historian Marc Bloch put it this way: when we see a man fall off a cliff we have no idea whether he was the victim of gravity or geology (crumbling ground).'

'This is the quantum world, one in which life is not predictable because physics is not either. Generals may not actually win battles any more than politicians run countries or inventors make breakthroughs. Individuals may make a difference, leadership still matters, but there is no reason to conclude that because a battle is won that a general won it. An army might fold because it is simply demoralised. In a highly complex world the very notion of "cause" is deeply suspect. History is not entirely the result of purposeful design; more often than not causes are emergent, collective, inexorable forces, or events simply "happen" because of ill luck or chance.' (Ridley, 2015, 5).

'And that', adds the General, 'is why I broke with Machiavelli. I was impressed with his book *The Prince*. Like his book mine was intended as a guide to action; like him I put particular emphasis on historical understanding. He claimed to have set out a theory of war though he didn't call it that: he spoke of "an untrodden path", not of a methodology. And his method—historical analysis—was anything but methodical. But whereas he set out to produce a set of universal principles I set out more modestly to provide my readers with some practical heuristics, or rules of thumb, precisely because I knew that history is not an infallible source of "good" and "bad" practices. Unlike natural science, where an event is usually the same as another—a stone rolling down a hill usually picks up speed as it arrives at the bottom, thanks to the law of gravity—historical events are not governed by laws. Human beings to begin with are not logical but rational, and to be rational also means to be open to passions and emotions of which one may not always be aware. And even when they try to be rational they often act unreasonably because they are not always able to judge what is really in their best interests.'

'In the *Discourses*,' adds Lindeman, 'Machiavelli does acknowledge that even his own rules can lead to defeat—a general who observes them may win; another who is equally faithful to them may lose.'

'Precisely', adds Clausewitz. 'And that is why he brought in to play two very unscientific principles: *virtu* and *fortuna*. Chance can never be eliminated altogether. Inductive reasoning from history is problematic for that reason. It is not just that the human decision-making is so complex; we are not "atoms" or "neutrons". We read history and draw different lessons; we read our enemies intentions and act in defiance of his expectations. In other words, events in history take place in the knowledge of one another's reading of it. There is intelligence at work which is not the case in the natural world. I was especially interested in the world of possibility for that reason—Napoleon could have succeeded in his invasion of Russia 1812; Frederick the Great might have lost his great gamble; gamblers can win; boldness can pay off.'

'Well, all I would add', remarks Lindeman, 'is that you connect with our age as much as he did your own. You are still running ahead of your contemporaries.'

'Not quite so fast,' remarks another guest of the evening, a visiting professor from Stanford called Gene Snyder, a faculty member of the Department of Cognitive Sciences. He is Lindeman's personal guest and he is clearly here for a reason—to provoke the General. 'We are beginning to model war mathematically with the promise of making it far more predictable than you ever imagined possible, largely thanks to data.'

Snyder beams. He clearly thinks he has Clausewitz on the back foot. 'In your book you expressed a concern that one day we would be able to conduct war by algebra. OK, so let's see where we have got with mathematics. Quite far, I would say. Thanks to the Tactical Numerical Deterministic Model (TNDM), a database derived from historical research we can now measure the rate of rifle breakdown in the Ardennes campaign in 1944 caused by rainfall, for example, and the combat attrition rates of Iraqi soldiers in the first Gulf War (1990–1), which finally triggered the surrender of the rest. We can now take past battles and write linking equations to establish, say, the effectiveness of camouflage and sniper-kill ratios. Testing the equations against a historical database makes it possible to establish certain correlations that allow us to predict certain outcomes.'

'What I am getting at,' Snyder persists, 'is that you were perfectly right to claim—when you did—that mathematicians had a very limited contribution to make to war other than in, say ballistics. But that was because you had limited access to data. We are more fortunate: we may not have enough data at present but we're well on the way to acquiring it.'

So Clausewitz adds: 'I see. In future you really will get to win every time.'

Snyder shoots back, 'That is not the point I am trying to make. Remember that while you insist that war can't be made into a science, you do agree that it is possible to master some of its uncertainties. The trick lies in understanding a certain probability bias while not mistaking that bias for a historical law.'

'Yes, that is quite true,' Clausewitz remarks. 'I was fascinated by the laws of probability that could be observed thanks to the available data which often produced more or less probable truths. In my chapter on "Method" in Book 2 of *On War* I wrote that an average probability will produce an average truth.'

Lindeman interrupts: 'Some would even claim that you were the first probability theorist in the military field. Anyway shortly before your birth the French mathematician Buffon published his *Essay on Moral Arithmetic* (1777) which laid the foundations for behavioural economics, evolutionary game theory and Monte Carlo statistical sampling among other things—so we are all on the same page here.'

'Thank you for that clarification, Professor Lindeman,' says Clausewitz, somewhat archly. 'Nonetheless I think my discussion of probabilities is still relevant today and is likely to remain so for some time. Let me repeat that what can only interest us are events that happen often enough to be open to some kind of probability distribution.'

'Let us take an example of the latter,' Sullivan chimes in. 'During the Great Northern War the allies fighting Charles XII were able to capture the Swedish port of Stralsund on the Baltic coast. Charles thought it was invulnerable thanks to the fact that it was surrounded by an impassable lagoon on one side and the open sea on the other. Then a strong west wind blowing for several days together lowered the depth of water below the fortifications to only three feet. A Swedish deserter revealed this to the enemy who sent in a force to wade from the sea, which went undetected until it was too late.'

'Interesting,' says Clausewitz, 'you can't really hedge against such contingencies, but then perhaps you don't have to—the capture of a fort here or there may be a useful tactical achievement but it won't win or lose a war. But the unexpected when it impacts on strategy can be catastrophic.'

'Take Napoleon's invasion of Russia, which you witnessed at first hand', Lindeman observes. 'Napoleon could not have anticipated an unusually hot summer and cold winter any more than the German army the following century could have anticipated an unusually rainy autumn which turned the roads to mud, and prevented it from getting to Moscow. The problem is that Hitler had only Napoleon's invasion to go by and Napoleon had only Charles XII's in 1708. When it comes to rare events there is no "typical" failure or "typical" success, which is why it is impossible to assign a probability distribution to them.'

'Thanks for the history lesson, Bob,' says Snyder. 'But I am talking about something called "Big Data" and once we can use it theories like yours may be rendered obsolete. Read Chris Anderson's article for *Wired*, "The End of Theory", on the "Petabyte Age".' (Anderson, 2008).

'What's a petabyte?', Clausewitz asks, not unreasonably. 'It's 10^{15} bytes of data (or 1m gigabytes).' 'Well,' says Clausewitz, 'mathematics was never my strong point.' 'It doesn't matter,' replies Snyder. 'What Anderson tells us is that your way of thinking—well, our way too until quite recently—is on the way out. With enough data the numbers will speak for themselves. Petabytes will allow us to make predictions on the basis that "correlation is enough." We won't need theories like yours to understand the world. We'll soon have generalizable rules about how the world works.' (Mayer-Schonberger and Cukier, 2013, 71).

'Of course.' pipes up Lindeman, 'But you know very well, Gene, that Big Data as a concept is itself highly theoretical. It relies on statistical and mathematical theories.'

'You're right. I wouldn't set too much store by Anderson's theory myself and I am the first to admit that it is highly theoretical. Anderson may have been a little carried away, I concede, but he still has a point. Big Data may still be theoretical for now, but when it arrives it will represent a complete break with our traditional way of theorising. We are steadily building up a vast store of information that once analysed will shed light on social dynamics. Naturally this will require some technical skills and imagination—a Big Data "mind-set", you might say (Mayer-Schonberger and Cukier, 2013, 192). But the payoffs will be great. Indeed, there won't be much call in the future for military history and what it tells us or purports to about causation.'

'We've had this argument before,' Lindeman ripostes. 'Turning data into knowledge is far more difficult that you think. The point is that much of the data that is coming in won't be very useful but we may not know this immediately; we may discover this only over time.'

'I concede the point', Snyder says rather tetchily. 'But with Big Data I predict that this could change. Don't despair, General. We won't be able to use data to establish causality. It is difficult, if not impossible, to express causal relationships with equations (Mayer-Schomberger and Cukier, 2013, 65). That's why we still rely on intuitive reasoning. But with Big Data we won't be trying to identify causes at all; we will be looking instead for correlations and connections. And we will have the digital means to analyse relationships with much more confidence.'

At this point, Clausewitz shakes his head. 'What worries me most is that there would seem to be no place for humanity in all of this. War surely is the ultimate human activity precisely because it embodies the fight against our own contingency. And the contingent world is one of chance.'

Jones seems to have had quite enough of this three-way conversation. 'Can we get back to specifics, and to history? I take issue with you on one front: you seem to have understood everything about eighteenth century warfare except perhaps what matters most: it was in

deadly earnest. You tended to dismiss the wars before the French revolution as "cabinet wars" in which aristocratic regimes scored points off
each other but were rarely in earnest when they went to war. One
historian insists that your representation of eighteenth century wars as
bloodless is simply perverse. Perhaps, he speculates, you mistook style
for substance. The Baroque linear formations of the eighteenth century
and its rococo exuberance you chose to see as largely unreal compared
with the romantic energy and enthusiasm of armies led by Napoleon
(Black). You largely ignored the fact that Frederick the Great's Europe
resembled a piranha tank.'

'Perhaps, as it recedes history comes into greater focus', Lindeman
volunteers in an emollient fashion. 'I don't think the General is a man
who takes criticism lightly. After all, the balance of power did signifi-
cantly change in the course of the century; thanks entirely to war. It
witnessed your own nation's rise and the emergence of Russia as a
great European power, not to mention the progressive weakening of
French power in the years immediately before the Revolution.'

'You have also been accused,' adds Jones, 'of misrepresenting war by
insisting that the defensive is usually less decisive than the offensive.'

Clausewitz again, 'Well to that particular charge I plead *nolo conten-
dere*. I recognised that if I did not live to complete the revision of my
work it would be the subject of "endless misinterpretation." But a
superficial reading of *On War* will show that I devoted one book (Book
6) covering 162 pages to defence, and another (Book 7) comprising
only 50 pages to the attack. To be sure the second is shorter, in part
because attack and defence cannot exist without each other; the two
processes are interlinked, but I confess I have always had a bias towards
defensive warfare. I like to think of them in terms of language—
defence is about denying the enemy the right to win the argument;
attack offers you the right to push your own point home. In both cases,
the intention is to achieve a decision (*On War*, 7, 1). I always stressed
that defence was the stronger form of war with a "negative" purpose,
offence with a "positive" purpose. When you over privilege one you
may find yourself in trouble.'

'Quite so', remarks Jones. 'Take the example of France in the run-
up to the First World War. French military doctrine, unfortunately,
responded to losing a defensive war in 1870 by insisting that the army

should always take the offensive. One military manual of the time even claimed that battles were moral struggles determined by the will to assert oneself (Gat, 1992, 166). This is all very metaphysical and I don't hold with metaphysics.'

'Of course you would see that the cult of the offensive was a vivid reflection of your claim that war is a province of social life. It's to be found in Renan's lectures at the Sorbonne on the Nation-State: a nation existed, he insisted only because of the will of the people that it should, and that its will would be tested from time to time in battle. It's to be found in the philosophy of Henri Bergson and his concept of the *elan vital*: will is the compulsion to create, but only in opposition to a movement opposed to it. The offensive spirit, therefore, required "excess". When the French saw where that landed them in the First World War they retreated once again to a defensive mentality, to the Maginot Line.'

'Anyway, I would like to ask General Clausewitz a very specific question about what we used to call the "Great Man" principle of history. The Napoleonic era was nothing if not heroic in your eyes; in your portrayal of Napoleon we see one of those men who, in Thomas Hardy's words, "consumed themselves/To light the Earth". We also find a man who never saw life as other than a drama with himself in the leading role. General, you were called the "high priest of Napoleon" (a term that was coined either by one of your great admirers, J. F. C. Fuller, or one of your greatest critics, our illustrious founder Liddell Hart).'

'One of the most perceptive historians of the 1812 invasion thinks that Napoleon actually fought "a cabinet war" for strictly limited ends, not entirely dissimilar—somewhat ironically—from the pre-revolutionary wars that you so much disparaged. Napoleon simply could not comprehend that once he crossed the frontier he would be engaged in a total war that could only end in the total submission of one or other of the parties. It was seen from the first by the Russians as an apocalyptic struggle between good and evil. In the minds of its other principal protagonist Tsar Alexander it was a "war to end war". He hoped that Napoleon's defeat would help banish war from political life. The stakes simply didn't get higher than this.'

'And here is another thing. Although you yourself were present during Napoleon's invasion you seem to have been largely unaware why Russia eventually won through. Your own country might have needed military reforms to beat Napoleon after 1807; Russia didn't. It was able to take on the French without any fundamental change at all and it was able to do so because it was a vibrant society which had always promoted men of talent. The strategy of withdrawing into the country in 1812 relied on more than good luck and a catastrophic winter; it demanded a complex administration and the provisioning of food and horses, and a cruel but widely tolerated conscription service. Above all Russian society was strong enough to accept such a strategy without fear of revolution. The 1812 invasion all told was a colossal gamble, rather than a calculated risk (Lieven, 2014). It was in fact unthinkable, which is probably why he mounted it: he simply lacked the imagination to realise that it couldn't be pulled off.'

'You see', continues Jones, 'Napoleon's career explains war's continuing pull on our emotional life. There is a passage in Saul Bellow's short story "Mosby's Memoirs" which catches the continuing attraction of the Napoleonic Age. Mosby is a rather shallow figure in Bellow's tale, but he is surely onto something when he remarks (do you mind if I read the passage?—I brought it with me): "the Napoleonic dream itself belonged to an archaic category of personal ambitions, feudal ideas of war … The commander at the head of armies—nothing rational to recommend it. Society increasingly rational in its organisation did not need it; but humankind evidently desired it. War is a luxurious pleasure. Grant the first premise of hedonism and you must accept the rest also. Rational foundations of modernity are cunningly accepted by man as the launching platform of ever wilder irrationalities." (Bellow, 1969, 167). Quite so—the appeal of the invasion, like the appeal of war, is precisely its irrationality'.

Clausewitz seems unimpressed. 'I think you are being a little unfair, you know. I did explain why Napoleon ultimately fell—he pushed his luck too far. Don't you recall the very last sentence of my book? "The man who sacrifices the possible for the impossible is a fool".' (*On War*, 8, 9)

Agreed, adds Jones, 'but that is only the half of it. He was also an arch-centraliser. If Europe was becoming nationalist, embryonic nation-states were bound to go their own way. Centripetal forces are not necessarily better that centrifugal ones. In nuclear physics, fusion and fission are both explosive. Napoleon's empire was an experiment in fusion that blew up in his face. The slow emergence of the nation-states especially as you know in Germany would end a hundred years later in an even bigger bang.'

'Even so', Clausewitz comes back, 'I did note that in the end he lost sight of politics altogether. He can hardly be blamed for not reading my book which was not yet written, but he can be blamed for not understanding my critical point that war is a continuation of politics by other means.' (Blanning, 1996, 271).

Sullivan adds for good measure: 'For him there were no politics: all attempts to find a point at which he went wrong, such as the Spanish adventure or the war against Austria in 1809 or the invasion of Russia, are probably misguided for that reason. His whole approach to life was fatally misguided. Every point at which he might have secured what he had achieved from the Treaty of Tilsit (1807) to Austria's mediation in 1813, which would have at least kept him on the throne was thrown away. It might be said that he never missed an opportunity to miss an opportunity. Napoleon the self-proclaimed man of destiny fell in the end because he came to believe his own myth. What he forgot is that "destiny" is not the language of politics. When he spoke of England as a "nation of shopkeepers" he was really expressing his contempt for all who live by the laws of reality and conduct politics by the art of the possible.' (McLynn, 1997, 668).

'His eventual fate,' adds Snyder, 'is a perfect example of what we call the Peter Principle that in any organisation a person who is mediocre but competent gets promoted to a position in which he needs to be more than mediocre. Then the promotions stop; he has found his level of incompetence. The Generalised Peter Principle has been adopted by scientists to explain that the more successful you are, the less successful you will become. Even in evolution systems tend to develop up to the limit of their adaptive competence. Everything progresses to the point at which it founders. The shape of existence is the shape of failure.' (Carr, 2013, 397)

I can see from their blank faces that the Professors are not too impressed by that argument. 'You wanted to discuss technology, I think, Mary,' Lindeman continues apace, turning to Professor Sullivan. 'Yes, you really thought that not much was going to change in warfare, as far as technology was concerned. I get it up to a point; you folks didn't know you were living through an industrial revolution and your own country was—how can I put this—left of centre-field in what was already becoming an industrial revolution.'

'The matter is a little more complex than that,' the General replies. 'I suppose I was sceptical about technological change for a reason. It had never transformed war decisively. Take the longbow which gave the English a tactical edge on the battlefield but did not allow them to hold ground—they eventually lost to the French in the Hundred Years War.'

Snyder interjects, 'Ah, but you see for technology to change things you need to apply science and governments need to invest in R&D and no state did that before the industrial revolution, did they? The Chinese back in the thirteenth century had gunpowder, the Mongols didn't, but you don't find the Song Empire setting up a Manhattan Project to save the empire by inventing a Doomsday weapon.' (Harari, 2014, 293).

Clausewitz looks puzzled but recovers himself quickly. 'You must understand that we did take technology seriously, it's just that back in those days we thought about technological change very differently from how you do now. How can I put it? We experienced more non-technological ways of living and acting in the world. We were not unaware that war had become more lethal with the introduction of standardised shot for guns, for example. We knew that there was little real hand-to-hand combat any longer, indeed that most of the violence was delivered from a distance. The most important innovation in war was the arrival of indirect fire, which can be dated back to Russian howitzers in the 1750s though this was not to be really revolutionary until much later (Bailey, 1989, 118). We were not unaware, in other words that technology was beginning to "structure" history.'

Lindeman chimes in again: 'Actually, you explicitly acknowledged that artillery had become the chief principle of destruction. (*On War*, 5, 4) A kind of early product endorsement, you might say! The historian Niall Ferguson claims that by the late eighteenth century the killer application of science had given Europe a truly lethal weapon: accurate artillery. It had experienced a "ballistics revolution" (Ferguson, 2011, 84). But Napoleon expressed little interest in technology, did he? He showed almost no interest in observation balloons, for example, or some of the technologies that could have in your words made a "quantum leap", like Fulton's submarine and steamboat. And this was the case despite his association with the greatest scientists of his day, like

Laplace who worked hard to keep the French army at the cutting edge of science.'

Sullivan asks, 'Weren't these anyway before their time? Wouldn't they have required breakthroughs in metallurgy that only arrived much later?'

'But I can't let you off the hook, General', Jones ripostes. 'Isn't it true that you were simply unaware of the technological possibilities of war that were yet to come; had you not been you might have had something interesting to say about its future evolution. Some of your contemporaries were perhaps more enlightened, or should I say more curious? You seemed to be unaware that the first military treatise on air power was written at the end of the eighteenth century by an officer; in your own army, as it happens. We're talking about hot air balloons for observation and reconnaissance of course. And even when you were serving in Russia in 1812 the Tsar commissioned another Prussian inventor to create the first "bomber force"—an aerial balloon armada that could drop bombs on the enemy from the air. (Laurence, 1999, 64). Nothing came of it, I understand, but for the requisitioning of a thousand Moscow prostitutes to sew taffeta into sections for the aerial craft.'

And what about the Perkins gun and the Congreve rocket? Those don't appear in your work either, do they? Even though Congreve's solid-fuel rockets were used spectacularly at the Battle of Leipzig (1813). And of course the British had employed them in the bombardment of Copenhagen a few years earlier in the first rocket attack on a city.'

At this point, Clausewitz has clearly had enough. 'Look,' he says, 'You know what happened when my contemporaries thought they had glimpsed the outline of history? Antoine Jomini did talk about the Congreve rockets and the Perkins steam guns "vomiting forth as many balls as a battalion." He also predicted that one day soldiers would be wearing armour and I see these days they actually do. But may I also remind you that he also predicted that horses would be wearing armour, too; he just happened to get the horses wrong, didn't he or do you think we shouldn't leap to premature conclusions?' (Handel, 1992, 5).

There's laughter around the room at Jones' expense. A well-aimed salvo if you ask me.

Sullivan comes back in: 'Can I introduce you to a term that may help to make matters clearer—your age was process-driven, not product-driven.'

Clausewitz looks baffled. 'It's a distinction made by David Simonton,' Sullivan continues. 'We are largely product-oriented; we focus on gadgets and machines. In your age the attitude towards technology was more process-oriented. A product-driven model like ours focuses on the optimum return on investment in weapons like drones. The strength of the model is that it is simple, direct and readily understood. But what is a weapon without the social structure to support it. Every technology is a function of social life and every weapon has a social history. Ultimately, product-driven approaches sell solutions; process-driven approaches make them happen.'

'Well, we were well aware of how technology as "a process" had changed our thinking about war,' Clausewitz concedes. 'Newton had introduced us to a clockwork universe, one of motion governed by force—the way that moving parts of a clockwork mechanism are driven by the pull of weights attached to ropes. We saw war in similar mechanical terms. It was a convenient way of explaining why things happen and how things change. Clocks allowed for military synchronisation, of course. And once units of time became standardised, that changed the way we thought about soldiers—we tended to think of them as cogs in a wheel (wrongly in my opinion).'

'Even so we didn't allow the metaphor to become confused with reality. There's always a gap (isn't there?) between reality and our description of it. It's a mistake to confuse the map for the territory, or the word for the thing it stands for. We knew perfectly well that war was not "force" alone, any more than I suspect it is information processing, a metaphor you seem to have embraced with such enthusiasm.'

'But I think the main difference in attitude to technological change between my age and yours is that for you machines make history, don't they? For us, they didn't. But please don't think that we were unaware that we lived in a machine age. Newton himself had depicted all of nature as a great machine. Our philosophers were even talking about the perfectibility of Man based on the efficiency of James Watt's steam engine.' (Sennett, 2008, 83).

'OK,' responds Sullivan. 'But remember machines can't begin to make history decisively until you have simultaneity of invention. And that is the whole point, isn't it? You didn't live in an age of sequential clustering. James Watt's steam engine was originally built in a workshop, not a factory. It was only when steam engines were fabricated in a factory that the formula, as we would say, became open-sourced. The Industrial Revolution turned a hand-craft industry into a factory one and created an embryonic machine tool industry that allowed new designs to come on stream very quickly.' (Heilbronner, 1967, 345). Anyway, don't feel too bad about it, general. Very few people are aware of the revolutionary social changes through which they live.'

'Time is getting on,' says Lindeman. 'And I know that one of our members who hasn't spoken yet, Geoffrey Warner, wants to make a point—very much in your favour General, I am pleased to add, since you have come in for some criticism this evening.'

'Thank you', says Warner. 'General, you have been criticised quite often for the absence of moral content in your work despite the fact that war as it appears in your book is largely a moral parable. Indeed, if you read your book attentively you would certainly think twice before going to war. One problem in our politically correct times is that you are quite unapologetic in arguing that from the rational point of view, you should be very careful how you conduct military operations. Let me read a passage from your book:

> Kind-hearted people might, of course, think that there was some ingenious way to disarm or defeat an enemy without too much bloodshed. Pleasant as it sounds, it is a fallacy that must be exposed. War is such a dangerous business that the mistakes which come from kindness are the very worst. (*On War*, 1, 1)

You see students today often fail to see what you are actually saying, and that is because you are coming to morality through the study of history.'

'Indeed,' says Clausewitz. 'War is such a dangerous business that it is a mistake to try to limit the use of force. If one side tries to be nice, the other will probably gain the upper hand. Then the first side will have to respond and in no time at all both will find themselves locked into an escalatory vortex of violence. Both will be driven to extremes. The fail-safe is that institutional constraints usually come into play; European states, Adam Ferguson wrote in his *Essay on Civil Society* (1755), had learned to mediate violence even against other states which they wished to defeat; the more advanced a society, the less likely it would allow itself to be ruled by passion, for fear that if unchecked the passions would run riot. The example I give is that the Europeans had long ceased to put to death prisoners of war. They had learned that it was imprudent to do so.

'I always maintained that the key to victory is not the "net body count"—the number of men killed—but the number taken prisoner. In the fourth book of *On War* I add that the loss of life in battle is seldom so disproportionate as to make a decisive difference between success and failure. What counts is the loss of morale. Courage and confidence tend to evaporate very quickly and with it primary group cohesion; when physical and moral energies are spent, the spirit of the mass is often broken. On the eve of a battle fear and anxiety can be set aside by the prospect of the battle ahead; once a battle is lost fear and anxiety are usually overwhelming. When an army breaks, it usually finds itself defenceless. In the retreat soldiers are cut down by the cavalry; guns are disabled or abandoned; units that find themselves cut off from the main force usually surrender. As I put it, "Victory gains substance after it is already decided."' (*On War*, 4, 4).

'Of course these particular examples will seem very dated, as indeed they are, but you still take POWs (including "unlawful combatants" in the struggle against terrorism). The taking of prisoners is still of central importance. They are the true "trophies of victory as well as its true measure." The logical inference is that soldiers should be encouraged to surrender, or at the very least, not be discouraged from doing so.'

'So,' adds Warner, 'here we find two vital ethical principles: the intelligent use of force; and that the real inhumanity of war can be attributed to an escalatory process based on a "reciprocal action … which must lead in theory to extremes." But let me return to the original quotation. For the sentence that follows is for me the real "takeaway": "The maximum use of force is in no way incompatible with the simultaneous use of the intellect." It is a small masterpiece of irony, if I may say so, though the irony doesn't exactly leap from the page. It lies in the difference between what is said—when you take a life think of the consequences—and what it plainly means. If you really want to limit casualties, get war over quickly and make sure that you devise a strategy which has a reasonable chance of success, all things being equal (which alas in war is often not the case).'

'In our much more sceptical age we feel conflicted about war's inhumanity. We tell ourselves stories, or to invoke the popular clichés of the day, we craft "narratives" in the belief that narratives win wars (when usually only weapons do). And irony abounds. Thus the *Economist* can call a deadly bomb like *Perseus* the "first humane weapons system in history" and *Prospect* magazine in the United Kingdom can call the US Army's 2006 Field Manual 3–24 the most humane counter-insurgency doctrine ever to be published; and Human Rights Watch can insist that only Precision Guided Munitions should be used in war. Soldiers we also are told in today's world must be prepared to become social workers, civil engineers, school teachers and boy scouts. (Maddow, 2012, 210). All of which spares us from having to ask the really embarrassing question—do we have such clarity of moral vision that we can kill with a good conscience? Or is the exact opposite the case: have we replaced killing in the lexicon of war with grotesque euphemisms such as "collateral damage" and "accidental delivery." I think I would be right in saying that you are counselling that we should go to war knowing that it is your our own actions which may come to constitute the greatest danger to yourself.'

'Thank you for that Professor. Thanks to my study of history I came to the conclusion that morality is a set of principles or rules of thumb specific to a particular society, or profession. Although I always insisted that most moral problems have arisen from specific historical circumstances and contingencies—for example from the need to restrain religious passions following the wars of religion in the seventeenth century; or the misunderstandings that occur when two different cultures go to war against each other. Getting to grips with a moral conundrum involves, at least in part, locating its historical source, and that requires us to think about the historical construction of the conundrum, and to take seriously the deeply contingent nature of the tradition that we call "the ethics of war."'

Warner nods his head. 'Ethics, like all value judgements, deals with questions that cannot be verified, or even tested empirically. Behaviour can, however, thanks to the study of history. The experimental method is vital in analysing behaviour because it is not governed by any subjective criteria such as gender, race or class. The question that scientists ask is not whether something is reasonable, but what are the reasons for thinking it may be true.'

Clausewitz continues: 'It is possible to "test" what is "reasonable" in war on the understanding that what is reasonable requires that it remain political and does not degenerate into warfare (a permanent condition of life). At the very core of my understanding of war is the idea of responsibility.'

Lindeman butts in, 'One prominent ethicist argues that a duty needs to be perceived in order to be followed, but it exists even if it is not perceived; it possesses its own independent ground of action (Jonas, 1984, 100). The point is that the responsibility to behave rationally in all our endeavours is not only an ontological grounding (as he called it); it is an ethical responsibility. The ontological grounding is our capacity to make choices; our ethical responsibility is to make the right ones (Jonas, 1984, 106). I suspect that you would embrace this position.'

'To be sure,' Clausewitz responds. 'My overriding concern was to prevent limited war from becoming "absolute." It is only through the study of history that we can understand how wars escalate, and find within war itself some procedural constraints—not those that moralists might consider "right" rather than "wrong", but those which allow all parties to a conflict to behave in an informed and rational manner. In that sense, my theory could be said to be "scientific" in the sense that though science has no methods for deciding what is ethical, scientists can at least observe what actually works.' (McGrath, 2011, 78)

'And although I was certainly not of the Kantian party in the critical respect of thinking that peace could ever be "perpetual", I agreed with one of the principal dicta of Kant's pamphlet, *Perpetual Peace*. "No state at war with another shall permit such acts of hostility as would make mutual confidence impossible during a future time of peace" (*Perpetual Peace*, 96). I insisted that you only win a war when the enemy is prepared to admit defeat. Remember also that in war the result is never final (*On War*, 1, 1). In other words, you only win a war when your enemy is willing to live in peace with you. Even Kant himself accepted that the vision of perpetual peace was more aspirational than real. Until such time as it was realised, reason dictates that we wage war in such a way that we ensure that peace remains within our grasp. We should never release passions and hatreds that cannot be contained.'

Warner adds, 'Kant also explains in *The Critique of Pure Reason*, if war is to be kept within bounds and fought for politically reasonable (that is, attainable) ends, it must be fought by rules that we can reason out, in part from reading history. He grounds this injunction on experience. For we have no way of inferring causal relationships outside experience. We cannot infer, for example, from a causal order of nature to a God who is the author of nature. There may well be an intelligent designer at work in the world, but if there is we cannot prove it. We cannot infer from the injunctions of God that we read about in the Bible any moral obligation to behave well. We can only derive moral injunctions from the historical experience of dealing with each other. Ethics, in other words, inheres in the practice of war itself. It belongs to that rare class of phenomena that are autotelic, bearing their raison d'être entirely within themselves.'

Clausewitz concludes: 'This is why I have very little interest in international law, and little faith in international lawyers (Kant, too, thought they were "sorry comforters" because states tended to disregard them, and still often do).'

And that, my friends, was the end of the meeting. The Circle broke up and thanked our guest, who refused a nightcap and returned to his hotel. Was he happy with the discussion? We can't say—we didn't see or hear from him again. But I think we gave him a good run for his money. The man who bombed was Professor Snyder. Big Data; correlation, not causation—this is not language with which most of our members are on familiar terms, or would even wish to be. But then I suppose they don't read *On War* in departments of Cognitive Science, or Schools of Quantum Mechanical Engineering, or Centres of Biocomplexity and Informatics. Yes, I have been looking up the new sciences in Wikipedia. Are they the future of war? Perhaps, but it wasn't the future that Clausewitz talked about at the Defence College the following morning, so I heard. His lecture was all about the continuing importance of "moral forces" and the human space of war, even if we are hollowing it out. Snyder, meanwhile, went back to the US and gave a talk at the Singularity University in their series *Programming the Future*. So who owns it? Perhaps none of us do. After all, don't the professors tell their students: "Killer-robots will soon be coming to a theatre of war near you"?

6

IF NOT CLAUSEWITZ, THEN WHO?

Cave ab homine unius liberi is a not-so-famous Latin tag: 'Beware relying on one book.' So should we still rely as much as we do on one book? Perhaps the fact that we are able to ask the question goes some way to answering it. After all, before the publication of *On War* no-one had ever asked the question before and since its publication there has never been a similar book. The trouble is that Clausewitz has few equals. His genius is to be found in the theoretical strength of his argument (though at times the theory is often confused), not in the language in which he couches his thoughts—it hardly sweeps us along (there are sentences in *On War* that you can't always find your way out of). It lies above all in his enquiring nature about a phenomenon that had not been tackled consistently before. Most of the great philosophers wrote very little about war, although there were exceptions, as I tried to show in my book *Barbarous Philosophers* (Coker, 2010). The point is that no-one before Clausewitz had aspired to produce a comprehensive theory of war.

Clausewitz got there first. He was the first phenomenologist of war; the first theorist; the first writer to conceptualise strategy around a set of first principles; the first to apply psychology to war; the first to apply the scientific method to its understanding; the first to use military history in what we recognise as a 'professional' manner; the first to situate ethics in essential structures buried beneath everyday experience; the first to understand war as an explicitly cultural phenomenon;

the first to recognise its 'evolution' in the absence of a fully developed social anthropology. What enabled Clausewitz to translate tacit knowledge into explicit knowledge is that he was both inside and outside at the same time. He had one foot in the world of academia and another in the 'real' world. He occupied a territory whilst loitering sceptically on the border, which is where the most intensely creative ideas usually originate. (Eagleton, 1987, 40).

If that is Clausewitz's genius is there any other writer that approaches him? In his book *The Soul of the Age* Jeremy Bate asks a similar question of Shakespeare, and proposes that there is only one: the seventeenth-century Spanish playwright Lope de Vega (Bate, 2008). Shakespeare wrote about thirty-five plays that we know of; Lope may have written 1,800, of which 300 still survive. In the range of subject matter, the multiplicity of themes and the richness of characterisation, not to mention the brilliance of his poetry, Lope de Vega may well be Shakespeare's equal. But the point Bate makes is that he fell out of fashion very quickly. England was on the rise; Spanish power was waning. The English language was about to go global; Spanish penetrated the Americas, but no further. Lope de Vega was not translated; Shakespeare went viral in the eighteenth century thanks to some splendid German translations. Lope de Vega's name disappeared from memory; Shakespeare's remained prominent in the popular imagination thanks to the music of Verdi, the paintings of Fuseli and the psycho-analytic writings of Freud.

Is the case of Clausewitz similar? Is his dominance to be explained by the fact that he was German at a time when the Europeans were becoming aware of what Peter Watson calls the 'German Genius'? The German moment in history gave us, in addition to Clausewitz, Kant, Hegel and Marx. Is his popularity due to the reputation of German arms before 1945? The Germans once liked to 'capitalise' war (of course they capitalise all their nouns) though the emphasis these days is on peace. Does Clausewitz's continuing reputation owe everything to the fact that the United States—the world's greatest military power—remains determinedly Clausewitzian, at least in its own imagination? And will this change with the rise of China, which on current trends may overtake the United States in defence spending by 2030 if not earlier?

So, if not Clausewitz, who? There is no shortage of contemporary writers, but they would all acknowledge Clausewitz to be in a league of his own. As for his predecessors, only two make the cut: Sun Tzu and Thucydides. One is Chinese, the other is another Dead White Male.

The Art of War is a major work and General Franks could quote it from memory. But what he memorised was a list of aphorisms, totally divorced from the context (and military tradition) which gave rise to them. He memorised a checklist or inventory, from which one can derive knowledge but not necessarily wisdom. 'Becoming wise is an act of knowledge,' wrote Nietzsche, 'the greatest thoughts are the greatest actions.' We can read Sun Tzu with profit, of course, but it you are a western reader, will you ever really understand him? Will reading him ever make you really wise?

The other problem is that of translation, which still continues to bedevil Clausewitz studies. *Traduir, c'est trahir*, or 'to translate is to betray', is an old French saying. *On War* has been translated into every major language except Esperanto and Klingon (the respective translations are *Sur Milito* and *lit Ves*). War figures prominently, of course, in the Klingon language; after all, it's what Klingons do. Peace is the word of choice in Esperanto, a language that was invented to unify the world, not divide it. Eventually, I suppose, Clausewitz will appear on Google Translate.

There are a number of English translations available, of which by far the most widely read is that produced by Michael Howard and Peter Paret (Von Clausewitz, 1989). Howard recounts the story of how he decided to translate *On War* when he worked with Paret in the War Studies Department at Kings College, London in the late 1950s. The text only finally appeared in 1976. But even their version has not escaped criticism. Take Clausewitz's most famous saying, 'War is a continuation of politics by an admixture of other means'. War, in a word is inherently 'political' and politics draws on all resources including military/economic and even social and cultural (soft power). But the word Clausewitz uses is *Politik* and it defies easy translation. Should it be translated as 'policy' or 'politics'? But even then, adds Howard, we do not solve the dilemma because *Politik* means more than politics or policy. Howard speculates that another rendering of the word might be 'grand strategy.' (Strachan and Herberg-Rohte, 2007, vi)

Let us face it: German is not the easiest language to translate into English at the best of times, but does the word *Politik* really present any more problems than the word *coscienza* in Italian, which can mean both conscience and self-consciousness, as in Hamlet's 'conscience does make cowards of us all'? The French word *conscience* can also be translated into two English words that describe two very different concepts: conscience and consciousness. The word *liberté* can also mean liberty or freedom. The English have to use both words to finesse their thoughts: they talk of the 'liberty' of the individual and 'freedom' of speech. The concepts in this case are fairly synonymous, though they are not equivalent. It is usually easy to establish the meaning from the context but this is not always the case.

Even in English there are difficulties. Take the word 'probability' which Clausewitz uses often. What do we mean by 'probability'? A property that inheres in an event (the probability of a coin landing heads first is 50 per cent), or probability as an expression of a degree of subjective certainty or ignorance? Unfortunately in the English-speaking world, and especially in philosophy (where semantics is all important), we use the word 'chance' for objective probability and the unqualified word 'probability' for both subjective and objective at the same time.

And here is another thought. As Strachan and Herberg-Rothe remind us in an introduction to a collected set of essays, *Clausewitz in the Twenty-First Century*, every generation reads *On War* in the light of its own understanding and so each has its own reading of the work. They go on to say that we read Clausewitz not because we are interested in the man but because we are still interested in war and that, of course, means we do not always tend to ask too many questions about what he meant. We are more interested in what we *think* he meant. We still read him—as we do all great writers—only because we find in him something his contemporaries did not.

All translation involves rebooting for that reason. To translate is to travel from one age to the next, as well as one language to another. As François Jullien writes, it requires the 'language of arrival.' A translation is not a loss; it is the opportunity as well as the means for renewed reflection—the chance to probe what an author's means in the language of one's own time—and here is the main point: to open up another possibility. 'Rebooting' Clausewitz merely involves taking him further. (Jullien, 2015, 11–112).

IF NOT CLAUSEWITZ, THEN WHO?

The good news is that no-one has attempted, at least not yet, a radical transliteration of Clausewitz's work. Plato has not been so lucky. The French philosopher Alain Badiou for example has published an edition of *The Republic* in which the order of chapters is reversed, the famous cave scene is transformed into an immense cinema, and one of the young men who address Socrates is transformed into a woman. Badiou even claims his version is more faithful to Plato than any other. But then there is that small problem of the title: we know the work as *The Republic*; it was not however the word Plato himself used. That was *Politeia*, which can be rendered as 'the state', 'the affairs of state', or 'the life of the people'. And for our purposes we should remember that Clausewitz thought that war as a continuation of politics involves all three.

If there is a problem with the Clausewitz translations, it is nothing compared to the problem of rendering an ancient Chinese text into English. Can you ever in fact hope to transcend the fixed lines of language and history? You can try, but I suspect that you will almost always fall short. Clausewitz inherited his methodological approach from the Greeks. The Greeks introduced us to essences and paradigms and the Greek verb 'to be', which grounded in a single word both predication and identity and thus allowed us to separate the concrete from the abstract (Jullien, 2014, 154). The Chinese language has no morphology—neither conjugations nor declensions—and classical Chinese has almost no syntax. It is not constrained to decide between genders or tenses, or even the difference between plural/singular. It is not forced to give the verb a particular subject. And because it is almost without syntax, the Chinese are given to thinking not of essences so much as of flux: the continuous, the transitional and inter-active. And where does Clausewitz's idea of war as a 'clash of wills' come from? It may come from language. In Chinese there are no tenses. It is possible to describe an action without revealing when it happened. In the Indo-European languages it is impossible. In the West we are all too aware of time passing, of the transience of military glory, of the urgent need to move on.

The Art of War is also fragmentary—it is even unclear what the text actually is. Great writers, insists J. M. Coetzee, deform the medium in order to say what has never been said before—they take the medium further as James Joyce did with the novel in the case of *Ulysses* and Foucault with the history of mentalities. But we don't know what Sun

Tzu's medium actually was, and we don't know the extent of his originality. The text we have may be a kind of primer, or set of lecture notes
for a readership that was expected to be fully *au fait* with the tradition
it represents. It is a book whose parts are greater than their sum. My
former student Derek Yuen has written a book, *Deciphering Sun Tzu*,
which offers an original interpretation of the text. But I believe that
one needs to invest enormous time and effort to really understand
what Sun Tzu is saying. And if students find *On War* hard going, can we
really expect them to delve deeper into Chinese thinking, especially
without knowledge of Daoism, the prevailing philosophical architec-
ture that underpins *The Art of War*? And here is another thing. You really
have to have a knowledge of Chinese military history to understand the
book, and this is surely asking too much of Western students. Even in
the case of Clausewitz few of them bother to read his essays on
Frederick the Great or what he has to say about the Thirty Years' War.
It is not that students shouldn't know about the Thirty Years' War—
they really should—but it is no longer taught in most schools. Western
students rarely know the great battles of their own country's past, and
many are hard pressed to name its great generals. In the case of my
generation the rhythm and cadences of major battles were deeply
ingrained in the national social imaginary.

* * *

This brings me to the only other challenger to Clausewitz. 'All of us are
mysteriously affected by our names,' remarks Paul, the hero of Milan
Kundera's novel *Immortality*. Would Clausewitz's writing have the same
qualities if he had been called Auguste Otto Ruhle von Lilienstern, the
man from he who has been accused of plagiarising? You may think that
this is not strictly an academic question, and you would be right. But it
is the kind of question a student might ask in a dreary seminar room in
a late afternoon. Only a handful of great men to be sure lend their
names to adjectives. You have to be lucky in your surname. Clausewitz
was certainly lucky in the cluster of consonants that gave us the word
Clausewitzian. But there is another name that also lends itself to an
adjective—Thucydidean. Thucydides was the very first military historian—arguably the first western political theorist—and there are a
number of interesting parallels between his life and Clausewitz's.

Neither writer completed their work—Thucydides died before the end of the Peloponnesian war, in which he served as a general and was later disgraced for losing an engagement. And neither were really cut out for success—Clausewitz was never really trusted again by the Prussian court after he resigned his commission in 1812, and Thucydides was disgraced for losing a battle. Neither man, in other words, lived long enough to outlive their times.

Both are also part of the American military curriculum. Thucydides has been on the Marine Corps syllabus since 1972 for his comments on amphibious warfare and the use of sea power. Whether those who read him understand him any better than they do Clausewitz is a moot question. After 9/11, wrote Victor Davis Hanson, Americans were more likely to believe a dead white Greek than the most sophisticated social scientists of the modern western world (Miller, 2004). The trouble is, as the classicist Daniel Mendelsohn later complained, the hawks on Iraq had a very basic understanding of Thucydides nine months into the invasion. They kept misquoting him or quoting him out of context; they simply refused to come to grips (let alone acknowledge) the subtlety of his thought (Leebaert, 2010, 205).

There are many reasons why students should read Thucydides. He was the very first historian to talk about strategy (Pericles, the Athenian leader may well have invented it—how did a sea power outfight a land power, and haemorrhage away the land power's strength? (Ober, 2014). Another American historian claims that he is the first writer to discuss tactics in his description of the Battle of Delium, where the Thebans used cavalry to outflank a phalanx and directed a deep attack at a particular point—they were apparently the first to adopt both tactics, just as Thucydides offers his readers the first clinical analysis of victory and defeat (Hanson, 2003, 231–8). But I want to focus on quite another theme.

Remember that he was a historian, not a phenomenologist. He mostly raises questions: Why do we often act out of character? Why do we commit atrocities? Why are we always pushing our luck? Instead of answering these questions he dramatises their reality. This is what he offers us—a dramatisation of war. True to his intention to write about the dynamic of war, Clausewitz does not make the catastrophic hubris of Napoleon the focus of his discussion. Napoleon's personality defects are pushed to the outer margin and made almost irrelevant. Peter Paret in his discussion of Clausewitz's essay, 'The Campaign of 1812 in Russia' (1823–5) makes an interesting point. Clausewitz is scrupulously fair in not condemning Napoleon for going for Moscow. It was, he insists, the right decision at the time. But even he admitted there was a probability factor operating. Once the die was cast, Napoleon was trapped (Paret, 1992, 113).

Today we might choose to explain Napoleon's failure quite differently: he should have quit while he was ahead. He should have avoided optimisation and learned to love redundancy; redundancy may even be necessary for long–term survival. He should have rejected the lure of remote pay-offs. And he should have put much less emphasis on past success. Both the contingent and the improbable become more important over time. As today's financiers have discovered, 'stress testing' and 'scenario analysis' both based on past results are often unreliable; past success can be deceiving. The more you rely on the methods you have pursued so far the more atypical your past success will seem (Taleb, 2015).

Thucydides didn't think of war in these twenty-first-century terms and I suspect that even had he been able to grasp them he would have been unimpressed. His intention was quite different. He was writing a tragedy in prose and would have made the invasion of Russia into a morality tale, as he did the famous Athenian expedition to Sicily (415 BC) and the punitive expedition to the island state of Melos.

We still read Thucydides, however, for another reason entirely. It is the emotional register of his work that makes it so different from Clausewitz's magnum opus. Back in 1943 the American psychologist Abraham Maslow drew up a hierarchy of human needs. They included, as one might expect, security, food, and self-actualisation. What is surprising is that he defined self-actualisation as 'meaningfulness', and went on to insist that self-actualisation can often pre-empt security for some. Take the early Christian martyrs who died testifying to the truth of their faith, or the first crusaders who abandoned family and possessions to liberate Jerusalem. Obsessed as we are with our understanding of security, the idea of finding meaning in death seems ridiculous, which is why we find young Jihadists so mystifying and terrifying at the same time.

Why do they join up? We don't really know any more than we know why people become serial killers. Not once has the FBI profiling unit in Quantico, Virginia instigated the arrest of a serial killer; it is only after their capture that we are we told that that they 'fit' the FBI profile. The same is probably true of profiling today's jihadists. They come from poor countries and the wealthiest in the world; they come from both liberal democracies and authoritarian states. We don't have sufficient knowledge or imagination to capture the phenomenon. But boredom is probably an important factor. Freed from the predictable and controlled they can render their lives meaningful for the first time. And that is true not only of those who have joined ISIS, but also members of Danish biker gangs who have gone out to support Kurdish fighters against Islamic State. Websites with a Fundamentalist Christian orientation have started to talk of a 'crusade' or 'reverse jihad' against the same movements.

But before we despair of understanding the phenomenon, read Thucydides. 'There were great numbers of young men who had never been in a war and were consequently far from unwilling to join in this one.' This quote from his *History* is inscribed on the walls of the Imperial War Museum in London because it tells you so much about the reasons wars happen and about the nature of men. And though a generation nurtured on First World War poetry may find this surprising, it really isn't. Many young men may not make it back, or may return home disillusioned, or may be committed to prison, but for a lucky few it is everything they hoped it would be and more. 'It was better than Call of Duty' was the rather pathetic message a father left his family when he joined ISIS—he was the first British jihadist to blow himself up in Iraq. (Jaber and Kerbaj, 2014)

Peter Toohey argues that boredom is a term that masks a constellation of independent disorders, including frustration and depression. And boredom can grow rancid very quickly, and turn into a toxic mix of resentment and general malice. The flight into Jihadism is not exactly transcendent but at least it offers some kind of escape. And what that escape requires is to move from the alienation of being alone to the joy of being a member of a group (Toohey, 2014). In his book *Talking to the Enemy*, Scott Atran insists that most Jihadists are far less interested in religion than in identity-fusion, academic speak for group solidarity (Atran, 2010). Technology has put them in touch with each other—they are both isolated and wired in at the same time. It is all so 'cool'. The same group dynamics applied to young Danes, Norwegians and Dutchmen who joined the Waffen SS in the Second World War, not because of the ideology but because of the Hugo Boss uniforms, the still-compelling Nazi aesthetic. Thanks to technology you can act these days in your own snuff movie with the 'money-shot' being the beheading. You can employ the gangster slang of the gangs with which you hang out in Bradford, or East London, which is cooler still. You can strut, preen, dress up and terrify Westerners, and it is all ideologically permitted.

Thucydides had an insight into such behaviour; Clausewitz didn't. The monsters were certainly out there in Napoleonic Europe, in the small wars that the French found themselves fighting, but they were beyond the horizon of both his culture and his imagination. They weren't beyond Shakespeare's, but then what was? In *King Lear* Albany says, 'It will come/humanity must perforce prey on itself/like monsters of the deep.' Here is Nietzsche asking in *Also Spracht Zarathustra*: 'Still is the bottom of the sea: who would guess that it harbours so many sportive monsters?' Or, if you want to be more prosaic, here is Captain Barbossa in *Pirates of the Caribbean:* 'You're off the edge of the map, mate. Here there be monsters.'

And here is Thucydides, reminding his readers that it is in war's shocking cruelty that we make out our own true image: 'Human nature, always ready to offend even when law exists, showed itself proudly in its true colours as something incapable of controlling passion, insubordinate to the idea of justice … [and here is the killer point] … the enemy of everything superior to itself.' (Barrow, 2007, 45). It is a rather sobering formula for those of us who like to invoke the term 'humanity' not only to describe a particular species but also the qualities which many of us still deem it to embody.

Whether he is writing about how war unleashes primal fears and passions or how ambition can lead to disaster, there is really no other writer who does justice to what the poet Pindar called war: 'the thing of fear'. To call war a 'thing' is to acknowledge its irreducible complexity. To call it 'the human thing' (*to anthropon*), as Thucydides did, is to acknowledge the complexity of human nature. War is to be found in our hearts, as well as our heads. It feeds off the imagination, the understanding that things can be other than they are. It is rooted in the human story. Thucydides was able to speak about it in ways that

Clausewitz only approaches obliquely. If both he and Clausewitz were writing at different times from us, Thucydides in this regard at least is much more our contemporary. He would not have dismissed the terrorists we confront as 'retro' or 'neo-medieval'—words we use whenever we wish to tell ourselves that our enemies are at odds with history, when really they're not.

CONCLUSION

Much though I admire Thucydides' work, it cannot rival Clausewitz's in its complexity. *On War* remains the gold standard for that reason. Like Thucydides' great *History* it was also left uncompleted. He spent a lifetime struggling to do so, knowing probably quite early that he would never see it published in his lifetime. All of which actually shows the seriousness of his intent. His constant change of opinion reveals a real wish to go as far as his intellect would take him. This is one way in which his life connects with his work—the struggle against social exclusiveness and narrow-minded thinking he encountered in the Prussian military is paralleled by his struggle to nail down war itself. Had he been a 'greater' thinker he would have told us what war isn't. That is to say his total self-belief would have been reflected in a work which wouldn't allow us back in.

This tour of Clausewitz's work therefore closes with a question, not an answer, and I am afraid there is no refund on the price of your ticket. Was there any other reason why Clausewitz never finished his book? Was it because he wasn't up to the task? Or because he was a born procrastinator? You get to choose, but I know which answer I prefer and it is none of the above.

No phenomenology can ever be complete. It can help us at best, to grasp something of the complexity of the phenomenon being studied, something fundamental, but it can never totally explain away what the author is trying to understand. It can uncover certain fundamental truths of what Clausewitz called the reality of war, but when uncovered the phenomenon can often become even more impenetrable. Even if this were not the case no one can capture war in its entirety because it constantly evolves. Clausewitz's book is best seen as a work in progress, as war should be seen too. Clausewitz and his era's way of warfare died together, but war itself still has a long way to run. And that is why I feel confident that whenever we seek to understand war in the future the next generation of students will continue to read one book.

But Clausewitz's failure to complete *On War* may have quite another explanation. Perhaps, it should not be seen as a broken promise so much as an inevitable failure to crack the 'mystery of war'—he refers to the word 'mystery' several times in the work. Can it ever be cracked? Could his contract with his readers ever be fulfilled? Clausewitz the born warrior never asked the question Tolstoy poses in *War and Peace*, for which Tolstoy criticised him by depicting him unfavourably as a minor character in the novel—an unthinking Prussian officer who wants to extend the war, and to hell with the damage and injury that will result. These German advisers, says Prince Andrei (who will be mortally wounded in the battle the following day), 'have nothing in their German heads but theories not worth an empty egg-shell.' Unfair to Clausewitz but it takes us back to the often unarticulated thought of some of my students that perhaps Tolstoy was right: perhaps Clausewitz liked war too much, or perhaps most theories are devoid of 'heart' (as Andrei goes on to conclude).

Or—and let me close on this note—perhaps theorists tend to dodge the unanswerable question because it is beyond theory. 'War', says Andrei, 'is the vilest thing in the world: men come together to kill each other; they slaughter and maim tens of thousands; … and then they say prayers of thanksgiving for having slaughtered so many people—how does God look down and listen to them?' How indeed?

BIBLIOGRAPHY

Clausewitz left his great work incomplete at his death. It was, in his own words, 'a collection of materials from which it is intended to construct a theory of war'. His wife published it between 1832–4. He had left Book 7 in the form of a 'sketch' and he had intended to revise Books 2–6. But Book 6 is still a quarter of the whole and Book 8, which is also called a 'sketch' by Peter Paret, is more fully developed and extraordinarily important for the contemporary debate. There is really no need to wade through the whole book but if you do then you will end up being full of admiration for Clausewitz and yourself—him for the sheer scope of his ambition, you for your endurance.

Even many professional writers read abridgments and there are two in particular that I recommend to my students. The one I have used for this book (and to which all references are directed by book number, chapter, and where applicable, section) is to be found in the Oxford World Classics series, edited by Beatrice Heuser. First published in 2007, it reproduces the core of Clausewitz's thinking which is to be found in Books 1, 2, 7 and 8; it omits large parts of Books 3–4 which follow a classical pattern of officers' manuals on the art of war (which of course is what the author originally set out to write). But I would also recommend the edition in the Wordsworth Classics series edited by Louise Willmott because you will find chapters that are not included in the Heuser edition. It uses the old Graham translation (1873) (revised by F. M. Maude), which is the one that the Americans first read, including the young Eisenhower (who tells us that he read the version three times in his early career) (Ricks, 2012, 42). This version is much more faithful to the German even if it is not as fluent as the Howard/Paret version which presents difficulties of its own for many Clausewitzian scholars.

Von Clausewitz, Carl, *On War*, abridged, edited by Beatrice Heuser, Oxford: Oxford University Press, 2007.

BIBLIOGRAPHY

————, *On War*, edited and translated by Michael Howard and Peter Paret, Princeton, NJ: Princeton University Press, 1989.

Allen, Barry, *Knowledge & Civilisation*, West View, CO: Perseus, 2004.

Anderson, Chris, 'The End of Theory: The Data Deluge Makes the Scientific Method Obsolete', *Wired*, June 2008, http://www.wired.com/2008/06/pb-theory/

Aron, Raymond, *Clausewitz: Philosopher of War* (trans. Christine Booker/Norman Stone), London: Routledge and Kegan Paul, 1983.

Atran, Scott, *Talking to the Enemy*, London: Penguin, 2010.

Avineri, Shlomo, 'The Problem of War in Hegel's Thought' in John Stewart (ed.), *The Hegel Myths & Legends*, Evanston, Illinois: North Western University Press, 1996.

Bacevich, Andrew, 'The Islamic Way of War', *American Conservative*, No. 11, September 2006.

Bailey, Jonathan, *Field Artillery and Firepower*, Oxford: Milton Press, 1989.

Ball, Philip, *Critical Mass: How One Thing Leads to Another*, London: Arrow Books, 2005.

Barrow, John, *A History of Histories*: London: Allen Lane, 2007.

Barfield, Thomas, 'Getting in', *The Times Literary Supplement*, 2 October 2015.

Bate, Jonathan, *The Genius of Shakespeare*, London: Picador, 2008.

Bateman, Robert L., 'Pandora's Box' in Robert L. Bateman (ed.), *Digital War: A View From the Frontlines*, Novato, CA: Presidio Press, 1999.

Bauman, Zygmunt, *What Use is Sociology?*, Cambridge: Polity, 2014.

Behrens, C. B. A., 'Which Side Was Clausewitz On?', *New York Review of Books*, 14 October 1976.

Bell, David, *The First Total War: Napoleon's Europe and the Birth of Modern Warfare*, London: Bloomsbury, 2007.

Bellow, Saul, *Mosby's Memoirs and Other Stories*, London: Penguin, 1969

Blackmore, Susan, 'Evolution by Means of Natural Selection' in John Brockman (ed.), *This Explains Everything: Deep, Beautiful, and Elegant Theories of How the World Works*, New York: Harper, 2013.

Blainey, Geoffrey, *The Causes of War*, New York: Free Press, 1973.

Blanning, T. C. W., *The Origins of the French Revolutionary Wars*, London: Longman, 1986.

————, *The French Revolutionary Wars*, London: Arnold, 1996.

————, *Frederick the Great*, London: Penguin, 2015.

Bloom, Harold, *The Anatomy of Influence: Literature as a Way of Life*, New Haven, CT: Yale University Press, 2011.

————, *The Daemon Knows: Literary Greatness in the American Sublime*, Oxford: Oxford University Press, 2015.

Bousquet, Antoine, *The Scientific Way of War: Order & Chaos on the Battlefields of Modernity*, London: Hurst, 2011.

BIBLIOGRAPHY

Boyd, William, *Bamboo*, London: Bloomsbury, 2005.

Brockman, John (ed.), *This Explains Everything: Deep, Beautiful, and Elegant Theories of How the World Works*, New York: Harper, 2013.

Broers, Michael, *Napoleon's Other War: Bandits, Rebels and Their Pursuers in the Age of Revolution*, Oxford: Peter Lang, 2010.

Brooks, Timothy, 'Conflict in Mongolia', *Literary Review*, August 2015.

Buchanan, Mark, *Small Worlds: Uncovering Nature's Hidden Networks*, London: Phoenix, 2002.

Buley, Ben, *The New American Way of War*, Abingdon: Routledge, 2007.

Burke, Jason, 'State of Terror', *Prospect*, September 2015.

Caines, Andrew, 'White Spaces' *Times Literary Supplement*, 10 July 2015.

Caputo, John, *Truth: Philosophy in Transit*, London: Penguin, 2013.

Caputo, Philip, *A Rumour of War*, London: Pimlico, 1999.

Carr, Nicholas, *The Big Switch: Rewiring the World From Edison to Google*, New York: W. W. Norton, 2008.

————, 'The Mechanism of Mediocrity' in John Brockman (ed.), *This Explains Everything: Deep, Beautiful, and Elegant Theories of How the World Works*, New York: Harper, 2013.

Cavell, Stanley, *The Claim of Reason: Wittgenstein, Skepticism, Morality and Tragedy*, Oxford: Oxford University Press, 1979.

Chamayou, Grégoire, *Drone Theory*, London: Penguin, 2015.

Chandler, Alfred D. Chandler Jr., *Strategy and Structure: Chapters in the History of American Industrial Enterprise*, 1962

Claxton, Guy, *Hare Brain, Tortoise Mind: Why Intelligence Increases When You Think Less*, London: Fourth Estate, 1998.

Coetzee, J. M, *Inner Workings: Essays, 2000—2005*, London: Harvill Secker, 2007.

Cohn, Carol, 'Sex and Death in the Rational World of Defence Intellectuals' in Nancy Sheper-Hujes and Philippe Bourgeois (eds), *Violence in War and Peace: An Anthology*, Oxford: Blackwell, 2004.

Coker, Christopher, *Barbarous Philosophers: Reflections on the Nature of War from Heraclitus to Heisenberg*, London, Hurst, 2010.

————, *Men At War: What Fiction Tells Us About Conflict, from the Illiad to Catch-22*, London: Hurst, 2014.

Cordesman, Anthony, *The Iraq War: Strategy, Tactics and Military Lessons*, Westport, CT: Praeger, 2003.

Corfield, Penelope, *Time and the Shape of History*, New Haven, CT: Yale University Press, 2007.

Crane, Stephen, *The Red Badge of Courage*, ed. Donald Pfizer (New York: Norton, 1994).

Crowley, Jason, 'Beyond the Universal Soldier: Combat Trauma in Classical Antiquity' in Peter Mineck (ed.), *Combat Trauma and the Ancient Greeks*, London: Palgrave MacMillan, 2014.

Daase, Christopher and James W. Davis, *Clausewitz on Small War*, Oxford: Oxford University Press, 2015.

Daase 'Clausewitz and Small Wars', 2005, http://www.clausewitz.com/readings/Daase/*SmallWarspaper*.htm

Dawkins, Richard, *A Devil's Chaplain: Reflections on Hope, Lies, Science and Love*, New York: Mariner, 2004.

Dempsey, Gen, 'General Dempsey Finds Military Lessons in Literature and a Zombie Attack', *Wall Street Journal*, 1 April 2014, http://blogs.wsj.com/washwire/2014/04/01/gen-dempsey-finds-military-lessons-in-literature-and-a-zombie-attack/

De Landa, Manuel, *War in the Age of Intelligent Machines*, New York: Zone, 1991.

Dennett, Daniel, *Breaking the Spell: Religion as a Natural Phenomenon*, London: Penguin, 2006.

De Waal, Frans, *Chimpanzee Politics: Power and Sex Among Apes*, Baltimore, MD: Johns Hopkins University Press, 1982/2007.

Dostoevsky, Fyodor, *Crime and Punishment*, London: Penguin, 1951.

Drezner, Daniel W., *Theories of International Politics and Zombies*, Princeton, NJ: Princeton University Press, 2011.

Dupre, Louis, 'Kant's Theory of History and Progress', *Review of Metaphysics*, 51:4, June 1998.

Dutton, Denis, *The Art Instinct, Beauty, Pleasure and Human Evolution*, London: Bloomsbury, 2009.

Duyvesteyn, Isabelle, *Clausewitz in African War: Politics and Strategy in Liberia and Somalia*, New York: Frank Cass, 2005.

Dyer, Geoffrey, *Working the Room: Essays and Reviews 1999–2010*, Edinburgh: Canongate, 2011.

Eagleton, Terry, *After Theory*, London: Penguin, 2003.

———, *How to Read Literature*, New Haven, CT: Yale University Press, 2013.

Echevarria, Antulio, 'War, Politics and the RMA—The Legacy of Clausewitz', *Joint Forces Quarterly*, No. 10, Winter 1995–96.

———, 'Clausewitz: Towards a Theory of Applied Strategy', *Defense Analysis* 11:3, 1995, in http://www.clausewitz.com/readings/Echevarria/APSTRAT1.htm.

———, 'Clausewitz's Centre of Gravity: It's not what we thought', *Naval War College Review*, 2003, 61:1, 2003.

Edgerton, David, *The Shock of the Old: Technology and Global History Since 1900*, Oxford: Oxford University Press, 2007.

Ehrenreich, Barbara, *Blood Rites: Origins and History of the Passions of War*, New York: Metropolitan Books, 1997.

Ellis, John, *The Social History of the Machine Gun*, London: Pimlico, 1976.

———, *The Sharp End: Fighting Men in World War II*, London: Pimlico, 1993.

BIBLIOGRAPHY

Engberg-Pedersen, Anders, *Empire of Chance: The Napoleonic Wars and the Disorder of Things*, Cambridge, MA: Harvard University Press, 2015.

Engler, R., 'Social Science and Social Consciousness' in Theodore Roszak (ed.), *Dissenting Academy*, London: Penguin, 1969.

Eriksen, John/Dilks, David, *Barbarossa: The Axis and the Allies*, Edinburgh: Edinburgh University Press, 1996.

Eriksen, Thomas, *The Tyranny of the Moment: Fast and Slow Time in the Information Age*, London: Pluto, 2001.

Esdaile, Charles, *Fighting Napoleon: Guerrillas, Bands and Adventurers in Spain, 1808–14*, New Haven, CT: Yale University Press, 2004.

Fernandez-Armesto, Felipe, *So You Think You're Human: A Brief History of Mankind*, Oxford: Oxford University Press, 2005.

Ferguson, Niall, *Civilization: The Six Killer Apps of Western Power*, London: Penguin, 2011.

Ferrone, Vincenzo, *The Enlightenment: History as an Idea*, Princeton, NJ: Princeton University Press, 2015.

Fleming, B., 'Can reading Clausewitz save us from future mistakes?', *Parameters*, 62, 2004.

Freudenberg, G. F. 'A Conversation with Gen. Clausewitz', *Military Review*, 57:10, October 1977.

Furedi, Frank, *Therapy Culture: Cultivating Vulnerability in an Uncertain Age*, Abingdon: Routledge, 2004.

Furedi, Frank, 'Precautionary Culture and the Risk of Possibilistic Risk Assessment', *Erasmus Law Review*, 2:2, 2009.

Gallie, Walter Bryce (W. B.), *Philosophers of War & Peace: Kant, Clausewitz, Marx, Engels and Tolstoy*, Cambridge: Cambridge University Press, 1978.

————), *Understanding War*, Abingdon: Routledge, 1991.

Gat, Azar, *The Development of Military Thought*, Oxford: Oxford University Press, 1992.

Geertz, Clifford, *The Interpretation of Culture*, London: Fontana, 1993.

Gerrans, Philip, 'Feel for you', *Times Literary Supplement*, 16 October 2015.

Gladwell, Malcolm, *Blink: The Power of Thinking Without Thinking*, London: Penguin, 2005.

Goldstein, Rebecca, *Plato at the Googleplex*, London: Atlantic Books, 2014.

Gray, Jesse Glenn, *The Warriors: Reflections on Men in Battle*, Lincoln, NE, University of Nebraska Press, 1998.

Gray, Colin, *Fighting Talk: 40 Maxims on War and Peace*, Westport, CT: Praeger, 2007.

————, *The Future of Strategy*, Cambridge: Polity, 2015.

Greene, Joshua, *Moral Tribes: Emotion, Reason and the Gap between Us and Them*, New York: Atlantic Books, 2012.

Gutkind, Lee, *Almost Human: Making Robots Think*, New York: W. W. Norton, 2006.

Hagan, Kenneth and Ian Bickerton, *Unintended Consequences: The United States at War*, London: Reaktion Books, 2007.

Hall, Edith, *Introducing the Ancient Greeks*, New York, Norton & Co, 2014.

Handel, Michael I., *Masters of War: Classical Strategic Thought*, London, Frank Cass, 1992.

Hanson, Victor Davis, *The Western Way of War: Infantry Battle in Classical Greece*, Oxford: Oxford University Press, 1989.

————, *Ripples of Battle: How the Wars of the Past Still Determine How We Fight, How We Live and How We Think*, New York: Doubleday, 2003.

————, *The Father of Us All: War and History, Ancient and Modern*, New York: Bloomsbury, 2010.

Harari, Yuval Noah, *The Ultimate Experience: Battlefield Revelation and the Making of Modern War Culture, 1450–2000*, London: Palgrave, 2008.

————, *Sapiens: A Brief History of Humankind*, London: Vintage, 2014.

Haythornthwaite, Philip, *Die Hard: Famous Napoleonic Battles*, London: Cassell, 1996.

Heilbroner, Robert L., 'Do Machines Make History?', *Technology & Culture*, 8:3, June 1967.

Heuser, Beatrice, *Reading Clausewitz*, London: Pimlico, 2002.

Hill, Andrew, 'Steve Jobs and the Perils of Leadership Listicles', *Financial Times*, 31 March 2015, http://www.ft.com/cms/s/0/3f0475fa-d3d3-11e4-a9d3-00144feab7de.html#axzz4JCnGNodo

Hillsman, James A., *A Terrible Love of War*, London: Penguin, 2004.

Honig, Jan Willem, 'A Brief Encounter with Major-General Carl von Clausewitz (1780–1831)' in Lebow, Schonten and Suganami (2016).

————, 'Clausewitz On War: Problems of Text and Translation' in Hew Strachan and Andreas Herberg-Rothe (eds), *Clausewitz in the Twenty-First Century*, Oxford: Oxford University Press, 2007.

Hood, Bruce, 'Essentialism' in John Brockman (ed.), *Thinking: The New Science of Decision-Making, Problem Solving and Prediction*, New York: Harper, 2013.

Hoyle, Fred, *The Black Cloud*, London: Penguin, 2010.

Jaber, Hala and Richard Kerbaj, 'Derby father is first UK suicide bomber in Iraq', *The Sunday Times*, 8 Nov. 2014, http://www.thesundaytimes.co.uk/sto/news/uk_news/National/jihadists/article1481606.ece

Jablonksy, David, *Churchill and Hitler: Essays on the Political-Military Direction of Total War*, London: Frank Cass, 1994.

James, Clive, *Cultural Cohesion: The Essential Essays*, New York: W.W Norton, 2013.

Jayakumar, Shashi, 'Biker Gang Chic and Reverse Jihad: The Other Foreign Fighters', *RSIS Commentary*, 215, 3 November 2014.

Johnson, Rob, *The Afghan Way of War: How and Why They Fight*, London: Hurst, 2011.

Jonas, Hans, *The Imperative of Responsibility*, Chicago: Chicago University Press, 1989.

Jullien, François, *On the Universal: The Uniform, the Common and Dialogue Between Cultures*, Cambridge: Polity, 2014.

————, *The Book of Beginnings*, New Haven, CT: Yale University Press, 2015.

Junger, Sebastian, *War*, New York: Fourth Estate, 2011.

Kagen, Fred, 'War and Aftermath', *Policy Review*, 120, August–September 2013.

Kamienski, Lukasz, *Shooting Up: A History of Drugs in Warfare*, London: Hurst, 2016.

Karp, Aaron, 'The Changing Ownership of War: States, Insurgencies and Technologies', *Contemporary Security Policy*, 30:2, August 2009.

Kassimeris, George (ed.), *The Barbarisation of Warfare*, London: Hurst, 2006.

Kaufman, Stuart, *Reinventing the Sacred: A New View of Science, Reason and Religion*, New York: Perseus, 2008

Kay, John, *Obliquity: Why Our Goals are Best Achieved Indirectly*, London: Profile, 2011.

Keegan, John, *A History of Warfare*, London: Pimlico, 1993.

————, 'Introduction', in Paul Addison and Angus Calder, *Time to Kill: The Soldier's Experience of War in the West, 1939–45*, London: Pimlico, 1997.

————, *Intelligence in War: Knowledge of the Enemy from Napoleon to Al-Qaeda*, London: Pimlico, 2004.

Kemp, Martin, 'When truth is beauty,' *The Times Literary Supplement*, 23 October 2015.

Keneally, Thomas, *Shame and the Captives*, London: Sceptre, 2014.

Klein, Gary, *Seeing What Others Don't: The Remarkable Ways We Gain Insights*, London: Nicholas Brealey, 2014.

Kluger, Jeffrey, *Simplexity: The Simple Rules of a Complex World*, London: John Murray, 2008.

Kierkegaard, Soren, *The Quotable Kierkegaard* in Gordon Marino (ed.), Princeton, NJ: Princeton University Press, 2014.

Kneller, Jane, *Kant and the Power of the Imagination*, Cambridge: Cambridge University Press, 2007.

Kornberger, Martin, 'Clausewitz: On Strategy', *Business History*, 55:7, 2013.

Kortlandt, A, 'The Use of Stone Tools by Wild-Living Chimpanzees and Earliest Hominids', *The Journal of Human Evolution*, 15, 1986.

Krause, Kai, 'The Uncertainty Principle' in John Brockman (ed.), *This Idea Must Die: Scientific Theories That Are Blocking Progress*, New York: Harper Perennial, 2015.

Lakoff, George and Rafael Nunez, 'The Metaphorical Structure of Mathematics: Sketching out Cognitive Foundations for a Mind-Based Mathematics', in Lyn D. English (ed.), *Mathematical Reasoning: Analogies, Metaphors and Images*, London: Earlbaum Associates, 1997.

BIBLIOGRAPHY

Laurence, Philip, *Modernity in War: The Creed of Absolute Violence*, London: Palgrave, 1999.

Lebow, Richard, *The Tragic Vision of Politics: Ethics, Interests and Orders*, Cambridge: Cambridge University Press, 2003.

————, *A Cultural Theory of International Relations*, Cambridge: Cambridge University Press, 2008.

————, Peter Schouten and Hidemi Suganami (eds), *The Return of the Theorists: Dialogues with Great Thinkers in International Relations*, London: Palgrave, 2016.

Ledwige, Frank, *Losing Small Wars: British Military Failure in Iraq and Afghanistan*, London: Yale University Press, 2011.

Leebaert, Derek, *Magic and Mayhem: The Delusions of American Foreign Policy*, New York: Simon and Schuster, 2010.

Lehrer, Jonah, 'Don't: The Secret of Self-Control', 18 May 2009, *The New Yorker*,.

Lieven, Dominic, *Russia Against Napoleon: The Battle for Europe*, London: Allen Lane, 2009.

Lind, William, 'A Warning from Clausewitz', *CounterPunch*, 8 March 2003, http://www.counterpunch.org/lind03082003.html

Lindeman, Gerald, *The World Within War: America's Combat Experience in World War II*, New York: Free Press, 1997.

Lloyd, G. D. R., *Being, Humanity and Understanding: Studies in Ancient and Modern Society*, Oxford: Oxford University Press, 2012.

Lowrance, William, 'The Relation of Science and Technology to Human Values', in Craig Hanks (ed.), *Technology and Values: Essential Readings*, Oxford: Wiley-Blackwell, 2010.

Lukacs, John, *Historical Consciousness: The Remembered Past*, Wilmington, DE: ISI Books, 2005.

Lynch, Christopher, *Introduction to Niccolo Machiavelli, The Art of War*, Chicago: University of Chicago Press, 2003.

Lynn, John, *Battle: A History of Combat and Culture*, Boulder, CO: West View Press, 2003.

MacIntyre, Ben, 'The Bookshelves of Tyrants Speak Volumes' *The Times*, 22 May 2015.

Maddow, Rachel, *Drift: The Unmooring of American Military Power*, New York: Broadway, 2012.

Magenheimer, Heinz, *Hitler's War: Germany's Key Strategic Decisions, 1940–1945*, London, Cassell, 1998.

Marino, Gordon (ed.) *The Quotable Kierkegaard*, Princeton, NJ: Princeton University Press, 2014.

Mayer-Schonberger, Viktor and Kenneth Cukier, *Big Data: A Revolution That Will Transform How We Live, Work and Think*, London: John Murray, 2013.

BIBLIOGRAPHY

McChrystal, General Stanley, *My Share of the Task: A Memoir*, New York: Penguin, 2013.

McElroy, Damien, 'Mumbai Attacks: Terrorists Took Cocaine to Stay Awake During Assault', *The Telegraph*, 2 Dec. 2008, http://www.telegraph.co.uk/news/worldnews/asia/india/3540964/Mumbai-attacks-Terrorists-took-cocaine-to-stay-awake-during-assault.html

McGrath, Alister, *Why God Won't Go Away: Engaging with the New Atheism*, London: SPCK, 2011.

McLynn, Frank, *Napoleon: A Biography*, London: Jonathan Cape, 1997.

McNeill, J. R. and. W. H. McNeill, *The Human Web: A Bird's-Eye View of the World*, New York: W.W. Norton, 2003.

Metz, Steven, 'A Wake for Clausewitz: Towards a Philosophy of C21st Warfare' *Parameters*, Winter 1994–5.

Midgley, Mary, *Beast and Man: The Roots of Human Nature*, Abingdon: Routledge, 1995.

Miller, Laura, 'The Last Word: My Favourite War', 21 March 2004, *New York Times*, http://www.nytimes.com/2004/03/21/books/the-last-word-my-favorite-war.html?_r=0

Mithen, Steven, *The Prehistory of the Mind: A Search for the Origins of Art, Religion and Science*, London: Weidenfeld and Nicolson, 1998.

Mlodinow, Leonard, *The Upright Thinkers: The Human Journey from Living in Trees to Understanding the Cosmos*, London: Allen Lane, 2015.

Moore, Peter, *The Weather Experiment: The Pioneers Who Sought to See the Future*, London: Chatto & Windus, 2015.

Morillo, Stephen, 'Battle Seeking: The Context and Limits of Vegetian Strategy', http://www.acadamia.edu/449311/

Mount, Ferdinand, 'His Moral Glory,' *The Times Literary Supplement*, 21 August 2015.

Nicolson, Adam, *The Mighty Dead: Why Homer Matters*, London: William Collins, 2014.

O'Connell, Robert, 'The Origins of War' in Robert Cowley and Geoffrey Parker (eds), *The Osprey Companion to Military History*, London: Osprey, 1996.

O'Rourke, P. J., *Peace Kills: America's Fun New Imperialism*, London: Picador, 2004.

Orwell, George, *Essays*, London: Penguin, 2000

Osterhammel, Jurgen, *The Transformation of the World: A Global History of the Nineteenth Century*, Princeton, NJ: Princeton University Press, 2014.

Pagel, Mark, *Wired for Culture: The Natural History of Human Cooperation*, London: Allen Lane, 2013

Paret, Peter, *Carl von Clausewitz: Historical and Political Writings*, Cambridge: Cambridge University Press, 1992a.

————, *Understanding War: Essays on Clausewitz and the History of Military Power*, Cambridge: Cambridge University Press, 1992b.

————, *Clausewitz and the State: The Man, His Theories and His Times*, Princeton, NJ: Princeton University Press, 2007.

————, *Clausewitz in His Time: Essays on the Cultural and Intellectual History of Thinking About War*, New York: Berghahn, 2015.

Payne, Kenneth, *The Psychology of Strategy: Explaining Rationality in the Vietnam War*, London: Hurst, 2015.

'Pentagon Document Laser Battle plan Against Zombies' http://edition.cnn.com/2014/05/16/politics/pentagon-zombie-apocalypse/

Pepperberg, I, 'Tinberger's Questions' in John Brockman (ed.), *This Explains Everything: Deep, Beautiful, and Elegant Theories of How the World Works*, New York, Harper, 2013.

Pick, Daniel, *War Machine: The Rationalisation of Slaughter in the Modern Age*, New Haven, CT: Yale University Press, 1993.

Pinker, Steven, *The Stuff of Thought: Language as a Window Into Human Nature*, London: Penguin, 2007.

————, *The Sense of Style: The Thinking Person's Guide to Writing in the Twenty-First Century*, London: Penguin, 2012.

Pippin, Robert, *Modernism as a Philosophical Problem: On the Dissatisfactions of European High Culture*, Oxford: Blackwell, 2003

Plamper, Jan, 'The History of Emotions: An Interview with William Reddy, Barbara Rosentein and Peter Stearns', *History and Theory*, 49, May 2010.

Porter, Patrick, *Military Orientalism: Eastern War Through Western Eyes*, London: Hurst, 2009.

————, *The Global Village Myth: Distance, War and the Limits of Power*, London: Hurst, 2015.

Qureshi, Saqib, *Reconstructing Strategy: Dancing with the God of Objectivity*, Minneapolis, MN: Two Harbors Press, 2015.

Rappert, Brian, *Non-Lethal Weapons as Legitimising Forces? Technology, Politics and the Management of Conflict*, London: Frank Cass, 2003.

Rapoport, Anatol, *Clausewitz On War*, London: Penguin, 1982.

Reno, William, 'The Changing Nature of Warfare and the Absence of State-Building in West Africa', in Diane E. Davies and Anthony W. Pereira (eds), *Irregular Armed Forces and their Role in Politics and State Formation*, Cambridge: Cambridge University Press, 2009.

Ricks, Thomas, *Fiasco: American Military Adventure in Iraq*, London: Allen Lane, 2006.

————, *The Generals: American Military Command from World War II to Today*, New York: Penguin, 2012.

Rid, Thomas, *Cyber War Will Not Take Place*, London, Hurst, 2011.

Ridley, Matt, *The Evolution of Everything: How Ideas Emerge*, London: Fourth Estate, 2015

BIBLIOGRAPHY

Rorty, Richard, *Philosophy and the Mirror of Nature*, Princeton, NJ: Princeton University Press, 1979.

Rothenberg, Gunther, *The Art of Warfare in the Age of Napoleon*, London: Batsford, 1977.

Ryle, Gilbert, *The Concept of Mind*, London: Hutchinson, 1949.

Sartre, Jean-Paul, *Words*, London: Penguin, 1967

Shermer, Michael, *Why People Believe Weird Things: Pseudo-Science, Superstition and Other Confusions of our Time*, London: Souvenir Press, 2002.

Schlender, Brent and Rick Tetzeli, *Becoming Steve Jobs: The Evolution of a Reckless Upstart into a Visionary Leader*, London: Sceptre, 2015.

Schmitt, Carl, *The Theory of the Partisan: A Commentary/Remark on the Concept of the Political*, Michigan State University, (1962/2004); also available on http://users.clas.ufl.edu/burt/spaceshotsairheads/carlschmitttheoryof-thepartisan.pdf

Scruton, Roger, Peter Singer, Christopher Janaway and Michael Tanner, *German Philosophers: Kant, Hegel, Schopenhauer, Nietzsche*, Oxford: Oxford University Press, 1997.

Sennett, Richard, *The Craftsmen*, New Haven, CT: Yale University Press, 2008.

Sheldrake, Rupert, *The Science Delusion*, London: Coronet, 2013.

Shepherd, Ben, 'After a Fight', *Times Literary Supplement*, 17 July 2015.

Shweder, Richard, 'Moral Maps, First World Conceits and the New Evangelists', in Laurence Harrison and Samuel Huntingdon (eds), *Culture Matters: How Values Shape Human Progress*, New York: Basic Books, 2000.

Singer, Peter, *Wired for War: The Robotics Revolution and Conflict in the 21ˢᵗ Century*, New York: Penguin, 2011.

Smith, Rupert, *The Utility of Force: The Art of War in a Modern World*, London: Allen Lane, 2005.

Solomon, Robert C. and Kathleen M. Higgins, *What Nietzsche Really Said*, New York: Schocken Books, 2000.

Stark, Rodney and William Bainbridge, *A Theory of Religion*, New York: Rutgers University Press, 1987.

Steiner, George, *The Grammars of Creation*, New Haven, CT: Yale University Press, 2002.

Stoker, Donald, *Clausewitz: His Life and Work*, Oxford: Oxford University Press, 2014.

Strachan, Hew and Andreas Herberg-Rohte (eds), *Clausewitz in the Twenty-First Century*, Oxford: Oxford University Press, 2007.

Strachan, Hew, *Clausewitz's 'On War': A Biography*, London: Grove Press, 2008.

Strauss, Barry, *Masters of Command: Alexander, Hannibal, Caesar, and the Genius of Leadership*, New York, Simon & Schuster, 2012.

Stuart, Kelly, *The Book of Lost Books: An Incomplete History of all the Great Books You'll Never Read*, London: Viking, 2005.

Sumner, Mark, *The Evolution of Everything: How Selection Shapes Culture, Commerce and Nature*, San Francisco, CA: Polipoint Press, 2010.

Taleb, Nassim, 'The Fourth Quadrant: A Map of the Limits of Statistics', 2015, https://www.edge.org/conversation/nassim_nicholas_taleb-the-fourth-quadrant-a-map-of-the-limits-of-statistics

Tilly, Charles, *Coercion, Capital and European States, AD 990–1992*, Oxford, Blackwell, 1992.

———, *Trust and Rule*, Cambridge: Cambridge University Press, 2005.

Tooby, Jay, 'Rivalling Gutenberg' in John Brockman (ed.), *How is the Internet Changing the Way We Think*, New York: Atlantic Books, 2011.

Toohey, Peter, *Jealousy*, New Haven, CT: Yale University Press, 2014.

Toulmin, Stephen, *Return to Reason*, Cambridge, MA: Harvard University Press, 2001.

Trotsky, Leon, *Military Writings*, London: Pathfinder Press, 1971.

Tyerman, Christopher, *How to Plan a Crusade: Reason and Religious War in the Middle Ages*, London: Allen Lane, 2015

Van Creveld, Martin, 'The Crisis of Military Theory' in Gudrun Persson, et al (eds) *Military Thinking in the Twenty-First Century*, Stockholm, Royal Swedish Academy of War, Science, 2015.

Von Metzsch, Gen. Horst, *The Clausewitz Catechism*, 1936.

Voorhoeve, Alex, *Conversations on Ethics*, Oxford: Oxford University Press, 2009.

Watt Smith, Tiffany, *The Book of Human Emotions: An Encyclopedia of Feeling from Anger to Wanderlust*, London: Profile, 2015.

Watts, Barry, *Clausewitz, Friction and Future War*, McNair Paper 68, Institute for National Strategic Studies, National Defense University, Washington, DC, 2004.

Watson, Alex, *Ring of Steel: Germany and Austria-Hungary at War, 1914–1918*, London: Penguin, 2014.

Wickes, Robert, *Kant: A Complete Introduction*, London: John Murray, 2014.

Willingham, Daniel T., 'Smartphones Don't Make Us Dumb', *New York Times*, 20 January 2015, http://www.nytimes.com/2015/01/21/opinion/smartphones-dont-make-us-dumb.html

Wilson, E. O., *Sociobiology*, Cambridge, MA: Belknap, 1980.

———, *Anthill: A Novel*, New York: W. W. Norton, 2011.

———, *The Meaning of Human Existence*, Cambridge, MA: Harvard University Press, 2014.

Wilson, David Sloan, 'Why Dawkins is Wrong About Religion' in Alex Bentley (ed.) *The Edge of Reason? Science and Religion in Modern Society*, London: Continuum, 2008.

Wilson, Timothy, 'We Are What We Are' in John Brockman (ed.) *This Explains Everything: Deep, Beautiful, and Elegant Theories of How the World Works*, New York: Harper, 2013.

BIBLIOGRAPHY

Wittman, Gavin, *Eureka: How Invention Happens*, New Haven, CT: Yale University Press, 2014.

Wittgenstein, Ludwig, *Philosophical Investigations*, trans. G. E. M. Anscombe, Oxford: Blackwell, 2001

Wright, Evan, *Generation Kill: Living Dangerously on the Road to Baghdad with the Ultra-Violent Marines of Bravo Company*, New York: Bantam, 2004.

INDEX

INDEX

Avineri, Shlomo, 68

Baath Party, 98, 104
Bacevich, Andrew, 85
Badiou, Alain, 149
al-Baghdadi, Abu-Bakr, 104
Bailey, Jonathan, 136
Balkans, 80, 87, 89–90
Baltic region, 3, 90, 130
de Balzac, Honoré, 15, 83
banditry, 86–7
Banibridge, William, 81
Barbarous Philosophers (Coker), 145
Barrow, John, 154
Bate, Jonathan, 16, 146
Bateman, Robert, 54
Battle of Auerstadt (1806), 115
Battle of Austerlitz (1805), 85
Battle of Badr (624), 84
Battle of Balat ash-Shuhada (732), 84
Battle of Bautzen (1813), 5
Battle of Borodino (1812), 5, 7
Battle of Copenhagen (1807), 137
Battle of Delium (434 BC), 151
Battle of Eylau (1807), 52
Battle of Fallujah, First (2004), 87
Battle of Fallujah, Second (2005), 5–6, 75
Battle of Gettysburg (1863), 57
Battle of Hattin (1187), 84
Battle of Hunayn (630), 84
Battle of Jena (1806), 54, 85
Battle of Leipzig (1813), 5, 137
Battle of Lodi (1796), 55–6
Battle of Mutah (629), 84
Battle of Nahawand (642), 84
Battle of Okinawa (1945), 57
Battle of Poitiers (732), 84
Battle of Qadisiya (636), 84
Battle of Stalingrad (1942–43), 75
Battle of the Somme (1916), 57

Battle of Tours (732), 84
Battle of Trafalgar (1805), xviii
Battle of Uhud (625), 84
Battle of Waterloo (1815), 3, 15, 74
Battle of Wavre (1815), 5
Battle of Yarmuk (636), 84
Beaufre, André, xv
Becker, David, 12
Becoming Steve Jobs (Schlender and Tetzeli), xx–xxi
van Beethoven, Ludwig, 106
Behrens, C. B. A., 3
Bell, David, 117
Bellow, Saul, 77, 134
Bem, Daryl, 7
Benjamin, Walter, 5
von Bennigsten, Levin August, 52
von Berenhorst, Goerg Heinrich, 13
Bergson, Henri, 133
Berlin War Academy, 2–3, 13, 23, 40, 86
Beslan school siege (2004), 75
Bickerton, Ian, 105
Big Data, 130–1, 143
Big Man, 77
Bin Laden, Osama, xiii
Binmore, Ken, 79
Black Cloud, The (Hoyle), 8
Blackmore, Susan, 66
Blainey, Geoffrey, 44
Blanning, T. C. W., 43, 55, 135
Bloch, Marc, 19, 127
Blood Rites (Ehrenreich), 73
Bloom, Paul, 35
von Blucher, Gebhard, 113
Boko Haram, 82
Borges, Jorge Luis, 17
Bosnian War (1992–95), 89
Boston Consulting Group, 95
Boston, Siege of (1776), 53

174

INDEX

Bousquet, Antoine, 110
Broers, Michael, 76, 86–8
Brook, Max, 58–61
Brooks, Van Wyck, 77
von Brühl, Marie, ix
Buchanan, Mark, 108
Buffon, Georges-Louis Leclerc de, 129
Buley, Ben, 100
Bush, George Walker, 94, 97, 104, 107, 118
business strategy, 16–17, 95–6
Byzantine Empire (330–1453), 84

cabinet wars, 29, 132
Call of Duty, 153
Calvino, Italo, 91
Cambridge University, 125
Camp Bucca, Iraq, 103
capitalism, 79
Caputo, John, 125
Caputo, Philip, 8
Carr, Nicholas, 21, 135
Carthage (814–146 BC), 28, 39
causation, 33, 70–1, 124–7, 143
Cavell, Stanley, 38
centre of gravity, xxiii, 33, 112–14
Chamayou, Gregoire, 80
Chandler, Alfred, 95
Chandler, Raymond, xix
chaotic systems, 27
Charles XII, King of Sweden, 130
Chechnya, 75
Chimpanzee Politics (De Waal), 71
chimpanzees, 71
China, xi, xix, 16, 67, 74, 94, 136, 146, 147, 149–50
cholera, xx
Christianity, 13, 44, 94, 125, 143, 152
Clausewitz in the Twenty-First Century, 148

von Clausewitz, Carl Philipp Gottfried
  conservatism, 3, 4
  on culture, 59, 63–4, 115–19
  death (1831), xx, 80
  on education, 13
  on efficiancy, 13–14
  on emotion, 9–12, 49–52
  Eurocentrism, 83–5
  on genius, 4, 52–6
  militarism, 8–12
  military career, 2–3, 4, 5–8, 115
  on military history, 121–43
  modern relevance, xi–xxiv, 22
  and modernity, 12–16
  personality, xxi, 1
  phenomenology, 18–21, 69–83, 145
  on philosophy, 2, 4, 17, 19–20, 28–31, 46
  physical appearance, 2
  on politics, 10, 17, 19, 26, 31, 39–47, 63–4, 81, 105, 135, 147
  precursors of, 16–18
  on psychology, 10, 12, 21, 50–2
  on science, 24, 26–8, 123, 125–8, 142
  on small wars, 85–92
  on strategy, 94–120
  teaching career, xxi, 2–3, 13, 23, 40, 86
  on theory, 36–61, 99–100
  tour d'horizon, 64–5, 67
  translation of, 147–9
  versions of, xxi
clockwork, 138
cocaine, 75
coercion, 75–6
Coetzee, John Maxwell, 5, 149
cognitive dissonance, 31–2, 72
Cohn, Carol, 21

175

INDEX

Second Battle of Fallujah, (2005), 5–6, 75
Surge (2007), 87, 103
Isaacson, Walter, xx–xxi
ISIS (Islamic State of Iraq and Syria), 48, 77, 81, 83–4, 98, 104, 153–4
Islam Jihadism, 21, 81, 85, 152–4
Islam, 81, 84
Israel, 91
Italy, 55, 64, 76, 87

Jaber, Hala, 153
Jacques the Fatalist (Diderot), 15
James, Clive, xix
James, Henry, 83
James, William, 8, 34
Japan, 26, 42, 57, 67, 74, 76, 78, 107
Jaywalkers, The, ix
Jerusalem, 84, 152
Jihadism, 21, 81, 85, 152–4
Jobs, Steve, xx–xxi
Johnson, Rob, 66
Joint Chiefs of Staff, xiii, 58, 107
Jomini, Antoine-Henri, 10, 137
Jonas, Hans, 142
Journals (Emerson), 6
Joyce, James, 149
Jullien, François, 148, 149
Junger, Sebastian, 74–5

Kamienski, Lukasz, 75
Kant, Immanuel, ix, xv, 12, 13, 16, 20, 28–30, 46, 68, 142–3, 146
Karadzic, Radovan, 89
Karp, Aaron, 91
Kaufman, Stuart, 77
Keegan, John, xv, 10, 11, 63, 75–7, 84, 109
Keneally, Thomas, 74
Kemp, Martin, xviii

Kerbaj, Richard, 153
Kierkegaard, Soren, 47
Kiesewetter, Johan Gottfried Karl Christian, 28
King Lear (Shakespeare), 154
Kings College, London, 147
Kissinger, Henry, 88
Klein, Gary, 54, 56
Klingon, 147
Knight, Damon, 9
knowing what v. knowing why, xvii–viii
Kornberger, Martin, 96
Kosovo War (1998–99), 98
Krause, Kai, 126
Kulturlos, 59
Kundera, Milan, 106, 150
Kurds, 48, 103, 153

Landsberg prison, Germany, xiii
Laplace, Pierre Simon, 125, 137
Last Supper, The, 94
Laurence, Philip, 137
Lawrence, Thomas Edward, 9
Lebanon, 96
Lebenswelt, 11
Lebow, Richard, xxiii, 13
'Lectures on Small Wars' (Clausewitz), 86
LeDoux, Joseph, 52
Lee, Robert Edward, 57, 72
Leebaert, Derek, 151
Legion of Honour, 76
Lehrer, Jonah, 50
Leninism, xv
levée en masse, 14, 85
Liberia, 76
Liddell Hart, Basil, xxi, 121, 127, 133
Lieven, Dominic, 134
life-strategies, 50, 95

180

INDEX

INDEX

INDEX

INDEX

Schopenhauer, Arthur, 22
Schouten, Peter, xxiii
Schwerpunkt, 33
science, 24, 26–8, 123, 125–8, 142
Scott, Walter, 15
Scruton, Roger, 31
Second World War (1939–45), xvii,
    5, 26, 42, 43–4, 46, 74, 76, 107,
    154
    Ardennes campaign (1944), 129
    Battle of Okinawa (1945), 57
    Battle of Stalingrad (1942–43),
        75
    Normandy landings (1944), 5
    Operation Barbarossa (1941),
        43–4, 81, 130
second-order idiot plot, 9
self-perception theory, 7
Sennett, Richard, 138
Sense of Style, The (Pinker), 63
September 11 attacks (2001), 97,
    103, 104, 151
serial killers, 152–3
Seven Years' War (1754–63), 2
Seville, Spain, 87
sexualisation of war, 21
Shakespeare, William, 73, 146,
    148, 154
Shame and the Captives (Keneally),
    74
Shaw, Martin, xii
Shelley, Mary, xviii, 59
Shermer, Michael, 71
Shi'a Islam, 103
Shock and Awe, 54, 102
Shweder, Richard, 115
Siege of Boston (1776), 53
Siege of Toulon (1793), 53
Siege of Vienna (1809), 112, 135
Siege of Yorktown (1781), 53
Silicon Valley, 110
Simon, Herbert, 108

Simonton, David, 138
Six Management Lessons, xx
Skelton, Ike, 114
slavery, 79
Slowness (Kundera), 106
small arms markets, 48, 112
small wars, 85–92
Smith, Rupert, 89
Social Darwinism, 68–9
social media, xix, xxii, 83, 84
Social Network Analysis (SNA), 80
sociology, 19
Socrates, 149
Somalia, 96
Somerfield, Derek, 12
Song Empire (960–1279), 136
Sorel, Georges, 34, 90
Soul of the Age, The (Bate), 146
Southey, Robert, 21
Soviet Union (1922–91), xxi, 26,
    42, 43, 48, 57, 75, 130
Spain, 86–8, 90, 146
    Civil War (1936–39), 86
    Peninsular War (1808–14),
        86–8, 90, 135
    War of the Spanish Succession
        (1701–1714), 124
Spears, Britney, 94–5
speed, 106–8
Spirit of the Laws, The
    (Montesquieu), 30
Springfield, 78
Stanford University, 128
Stark, Rodney, 81
steam engine, 138
Stendhal, 15
Sterling, Bruce, 117
Stockholm, Sweden, xiv
Stoker, Donald, 15
Strachan, Hew, xix, 45, 147–8
Strategy and Structure (Chandler), 95
strategy, 16–17, 94–120

INDEX

INDEX

Army War College, xxii, 24
Civil War (1861–65), 57
Defense Research Programme Agency, 79
Department of Defense, 80, 96, 115
First World War (1917–18), 77
Gulf War (1990–91), 89, 94, 102, 114
Iraq War (2003–11), xiv, 5–6, 8, 32, 73, 75, 86, 87, 94, 96–114, 117
Joint Chiefs of Staff, xiii, 58, 107
Lebanon conflict (1983), 96
Marine Corps, 5, 71, 75, 93, 111, 151
military-industrial complex, 79
National Defence University (NDU), xxi–xxii
National Security Council, 21
Navy War College, xiii
Pentagon, 58, 93
Revolutionary War (1775–83), 53
September 11 attacks (2001), 97, 103, 104, 151
Somalia conflict (1992–93), 96
Vietnam War (1961–73), 8, 46, 74
War on Terror, xxii, 75, 80, 93–120
West Point, xxii, xxiii, 22, 23–61, 79
unknown unknowns, 109
Utility of Force, The (Smith), 89

van Creveld, Martin, xiv, xv, 14, 90
van Riper, Paul, 111–12
Vegetius, Flavius, xv, 16
vendetta, 86
Verdi, Giuseppe, 146
Vico, Giambattista, 18

Victoria Cross, 76
Victory, xviii
Vienna, Austria, 112
Vietnam War (1955–75), 8, 46, 74
Virgil, 70
viruses, 89
Voorhoeve, Alex, 79

Waffen SS, 154
war
    absolute, 31, 41, 42–3, 59–60, 91
    asymmetric, 28, 33, 34, 65–6, 91, 102
    and culture, 59, 63–4, 73, 115–19
    as dominant theme of age, 4
    as duel, 33–5, 80
    and emotion, 10–12, 49–52, 134
    escalation of, 26, 31, 41–2, 139–40, 142
    and ethics, 11–12, 60, 140–3
    fog of, 22, 111
    functions of, 79–83
    grammar of, 38–40, 44, 67, 82
    intelligence, 9, 65, 102, 109
    love of, 5–10
    mechanisms of, 72–7
    and misjudgement, 44
    mystery of, xvi, 69
    and narrative, 13, 30, 48, 58, 67–8, 82, 99, 106, 119, 141
    nature v. character of, 37
    ontogeny of, 77–9
    origins of, 70–2
    and politics, 10, 17, 19, 26, 31, 39–47, 63–4, 81, 105, 135, 147
    product-driven model, 137–8
    sexualisation of, 21
    small wars, 85–92

Milton Keynes UK
Ingram Content Group UK Ltd.
UKHW020639181023
430830UK00013BA/323

9 781849 047142